NEW VANGUARD 320

US NAVY PROTECTED CRUISERS 1883–1918

BRIAN LANE HERDER   ILLUSTRATED BY PAUL WRIGHT

OSPREY PUBLISHING

Bloomsbury Publishing Plc

Kemp House, Chawley Park, Cumnor Hill, Oxford OX2 9PH, UK

29 Earlsfort Terrace, Dublin 2, Ireland

1385 Broadway, 5th Floor, New York, NY 10018, USA

E-mail: info@ospreypublishing.com

www.ospreypublishing.com

OSPREY is a trademark of Osprey Publishing Ltd

First published in Great Britain in 2023

© Osprey Publishing Ltd, 2023

A catalogue record for this book is available from the British Library.

ISBN: PB 9781472857033; eBook 9781472857026

ePDF 9781472857002; XML 9781472857019

23 24 25 26 27   10 9 8 7 6 5 4 3 2 1

Index by Fionbar Lyons
Typeset by PDQ Digital Media Solutions, Bungay, UK
Printed and bound in India by Replika Press Private Ltd.

Title page image: please see caption on page 6.

Author's Acknowledgement

The author would like to thank Philadelphia's Independence Seaport Museum for its support in my research of *Olympia*, particularly Alexis Furlong, Andrea Pollock, and Hugh McKeever.

Dedication

For my beautiful wife Courtney Lee Herder, who accompanied me to Philadelphia and graciously indulged my nerdiness by climbing down into *Olympia*'s starboard engine room.

CONTENTS

US NAVY PROTECTED CRUISERS 1883–1918

INTRODUCTION

In the 18th century, the term "cruizing" referred to any warship operating independently. These vessels, regardless of their size or type, were soon dubbed "cruizers." Although this term could refer to any ship pressed into the role, performance and economics dictated that a medium-sized warship, the sailing frigate, emerged as ideal for this mission. By the 1870s, the term "cruiser" had come to refer specifically to the descendent of the sailing frigate, the steam frigate.

The period immediately following the American Civil War was an era of rapid technological change. As early as 1871, British shipbuilder William Armstrong realized cruisers could no longer mount wrought iron armor thick enough to resist the era's continuously improving naval guns. In 1879, Armstrong's Elswick shipyard in Newcastle upon Tyne received an order for a new Chilean cruiser. In lieu of heavy side armor, Armstrong chose to fit his new Chilean design with only a thin turtleback steel deck mounted low in the ship and sloping on both sides until it reached the hull below the waterline. This "protected deck" was only partial, leaving the rest of the ship unarmored. However, it shielded vulnerable machinery spaces from oblique hits and splinter damage, as the era's gunnery technology meant that direct hits or plunging hits from the most destructive shells were unlikely. Additionally, internal watertight subdivision would contain flooding outside the turtleback protective deck.

Armstrong's revolutionary new cruiser, *Esmeralda*, was completed in 1884 and proved an immediate success. *Esmeralda* was fast, heavily armed, and reasonably well protected on a modest displacement of 2,950 tons. This new warship type became known as a "protected" cruiser. A protected cruiser's design contrasted with the larger, heavier, and slightly older "armored" cruiser type, which was defined by an armored belt mounted along the waterline. *Esmeralda*'s impressive design inspired additional emerging navies to order their own protected cruisers from Armstrong; these *Esmeralda* derivatives became so pervasive that they were generally known as "Elswick cruisers" after the Elswick yard where they were built.

Across the Atlantic, the American Civil War's powerful US Navy (USN) had been allowed to fall into utter decay. By the 1880s Congress recognized the USN as a major security liability. Fortunately, the existing Civil War debt had been paid off, and US politicians became interested in rebuilding the US

The Chilean cruiser *Esmeralda* in 1884. With its partial protected deck, *Esmeralda* was the world's first protected cruiser. The first two US protected cruisers *Atlanta* and *Boston* greatly resembled *Esmeralda* in size and configuration. (Public Domain)

Navy, not only for reasons of national security, but for internal political and industrial advantages.

The old navy had been comprised of obsolete wood or ironclad ships, but in 1883 Congress approved four new steel-constructed vessels nicknamed the "ABCD" ships. The first ship completed was the 1,485-ton armed dispatch boat *Dolphin*, commissioned in December 1885. However, the remaining three ships were small *Esmeralda*-type protected cruisers: the 3,189-ton *Atlanta* and *Boston*, commissioned in 1886 and 1887, and the 4,500-ton *Chicago*, commissioned in 1889. Together, these four ships were the first steel warships built for the USN. The cultural and technological transformation that the ships brought in the 1880s and 1890s proved so total that the USN of the period is remembered as the "Steel Navy" or simply the "New Navy." Following *Atlanta*, *Boston*, and *Chicago*, the USN commissioned five additional, slightly larger protected cruisers between 1889 and 1891 – *Newark*, *Charleston*, *Baltimore*, *Philadelphia*, and *San Francisco*. Although broadly similar, each was of unique design and exceeded 4,000 tons. Finally, in 1894 and 1895, the USN commissioned three very large and fast protected cruisers – the two Columbia-class cruisers and finally the famous and powerful *Olympia*. These 11 protected cruisers formed the backbone of the early US Steel Navy. US protected cruisers served faithfully in gunboat diplomacy roles, saw front-line combat in the 1898 Spanish–American War, and then served as escorts and auxiliaries in World War I, before the last were retired in the 1920s.

The New Navy's protected cruisers can be considered a sort of "medium" or second-class cruiser standing in between "heavy" armored cruisers and "light" unprotected cruisers. Additionally, it should be noted that two cruisers from this period, the 3,182-ton Cincinnati-class cruisers *Cincinnati* and *Raleigh*, were often referred to as protected cruisers. However, unlike every other cruiser in this volume, they were designed specifically to be smaller than their predecessors and were often considered large gunboats. *Cincinnati* and *Raleigh* are therefore not included here, and it is hoped to cover them in a later volume on early US light cruisers.

US Navy protected cruisers are arguably the most famous cruiser type of this era for several reasons. The three "ABC" cruisers were the US Navy's first steel warships; the decisive 1898 Battle of Manila Bay was fought and won by US protected cruisers; and the famous Manila Bay flagship *Olympia* is the last remaining warship

USS *Constitution*, a 1790s sailing frigate and the classic "cruizing" frigate of the USN's original sailing navy. The steel cruisers of the late 19th century were directly descended from wooden sailing frigates such as *Constitution*. (NHHC 65-350-KB)

The United States Navy's first protected cruiser and first steel-constructed cruiser, USS *Atlanta*, as seen in 1891. The first three US protected cruisers employed considerably more sail rig than later cruisers, although still less than previous US warships. (NARA 512894)

of the Spanish–American War, surviving today as a well-preserved museum ship in Philadelphia.

This book is composed specifically to complement Lawrence Burr's 2008 New Vanguard volume *US Cruisers 1883–1904*, but without repeating it. For example, numerous books have been written focusing on the famous May 1, 1898 Battle of Manila Bay and flagship *Olympia*. *US Navy Protected Cruisers 1883–1918* will not ignore these important subjects, but will focus on less well-known topics, such as the Squadron of Evolution, and one of the strangest and most obscure US cruiser classes ever built, the 1894 Columbia class.

DEVELOPMENT

The world's first steam-powered warship was the US "steam frigate" *Demologos*, launched in 1815. Sceptical USN officers ensured *Demologos* (renamed *Fulton* after its designer, who had died that year) only saw receiving ship duty. By the 1830s, nearly 700 steam-powered merchantmen plied American waters, but none belonged to the USN. At the behest of Congress, the USN finally commissioned the partially steam-powered coastal defense vessel *Fulton (the Second)* in 1837. By 1842 the USN had commissioned two steam-powered paddlewheel frigates, *Missouri* and *Mississippi*, and two years later the USN commissioned its first iron-hulled warship, the Great Lakes sidewheel steamer *Michigan*.

The mid-19th century brought further technological developments such as screw propellers, rifled guns, and exploding shells. During the 1861–65 Civil War the USN peaked at 671 ships, briefly making it the largest and most technologically advanced navy in the world. Most of its fleet were steamers, including all 179 built or launched during the war, some 49 of which were ironclads. However, after 1865 the US government rapidly dismantled its expensive wartime Navy.

The USN had never developed a large, concentrated battle fleet, which American society associated with the imperialism of the great European

The Squadron of Evolution, better known as the White Squadron, viewed in 1889. From left to right, flagship *Chicago*, gunboat *Yorktown*, and cruisers *Boston* and *Atlanta*. The Squadron of Evolution was the first time in modern history that the USN focused on coordinated fleet maneuvers on the deep sea. (LOC LC-DIG-det-4a14155)

powers. Instead, traditional American naval strategy had always been *guerre de course* (commerce raiding) by frigates and privateers. Although a dubious strategy for winning naval wars, commerce raiding was suited to cruisers. In contrast to battleships, a cruiser's primary attributes were high speed, long range, medium armament, adequate protection against other cruisers, and the ability to deploy independently for extended periods of time. A cruiser was essentially the late 19th century's direct descendent of the wooden-hulled steam frigate of the American Civil War period.

By early 1881, President Garfield's Navy Secretary, William H. Hunt, would state, "The condition of the Navy imperatively demands the prompt and earnest attention of Congress. Unless some action be had in its behalf it must soon dwindle to insignificance." Fortunately, a $100 million surplus now sat in the US Treasury. That same year Hunt assembled the so-called Rodgers Board to study the building of a modern Navy. However, the reconstruction of the US Navy to revolutionary new technological and cultural standards would prove a complex and emotional national issue.

The Rodgers Board argued over whether the new ships should be constructed out of iron or out of steel. Steel was structurally superior to iron, and had been used successfully abroad, but there was much doubt that American industry could produce large amounts of high-quality steel in a timely, efficient, and cost-effective manner. The Rodgers Board agreed on little, but a majority report proposed an ambitious (if unrealistic) 68-ship program. More importantly, after intense discussions about the construction materials to be used, the board stated, "It is therefore the opinion of the Board that these ... vessels should be built throughout of steel." However, Congress remained divided.

More shockingly, in late 1881 Garfield was assassinated. The new president, Chester A. Arthur, removed Hunt as Navy Secretary and on April 12, 1882 replaced him with his own crony, William Chandler. However, Chandler acknowledged that the US Navy was "a subject of ridicule both at home and abroad" and he was motivated to continue Hunt's work. Chandler convened a second board of five officers and two civilians under Commodore Robert Schufeldt. More politically astute than its predecessor, the Schufeldt Board recommended only the two small, previous cruisers that had already been approved, plus three even smaller 2,500-ton cruisers, and finally a dispatch vessel.

An initial congressional committee proposed six steel cruisers and nine smaller ships, but on August 5, 1882 Congress approved just two cruisers, to be funded with whatever leftover appropriations the Navy could scrape up from its existing budget. The 1882 legislation was therefore effectively worthless.

According to Navy Secretary Chandler:

We unquestionably need vessels in such numbers as fully to "keep alive the knowledge of war," and of such kind that it shall be a knowledge of modern war; capable on brief notice of being expanded into invincible squadrons. It is well known that we have not the elements of such a force today. The condition of decrepitude into which the fleet has fallen through a failure to provide for its gradual renewal by modern ships is justly a subject of ridicule at home and abroad.

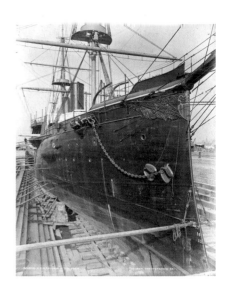

Protected cruiser USS *Chicago* in drydock. The black-painted hull is a mid-19th century USN style and reveals the photograph as preceding the Squadron of Evolution. *Chicago* was badly out-of-date when it came to steam power plants, but was fairly heavily armed compared with same-sized cruisers. (LOC LC-DIG-det-4a14155)

Atlanta-class protected cruiser USS *Boston*, in 1891. This view was likely taken during *Atlanta's* service during the Squadron of Evolution or immediately after the Squadron was dissolved in September 1891. (NARA 512892)

However, on March 3, 1883, Congress appropriated $1.3 million for the smaller of the two cruisers authorized in August 1882 (the 4,500-ton *Chicago*), while also funding two of the three 2,500-ton Schufeldt Board cruisers, plus a fourth ship, a steel dispatch boat. These four vessels would become the ABCD ships. Just as significantly, the legislation limited repairs to wooden ships to no more than 20 percent of the cost of building a comparable new ship.

The 1883 conception of the ABCD ships represents the beginning of the new era in the USN called the Steel Navy, or simply the New Navy. In addition to building new steel ships, the period saw an internal cultural and institutional USN revolution devoted to modernity and forward-thinking ideas, exemplified by the establishment of first the Office of Naval Intelligence in 1882, and then the Naval War College at Newport, Rhode Island in 1884. These augmented the civilian Naval Institute, which liberal-minded USN officers had established on their own initiative in 1876.

USN protected cruiser hull numbers, classification, and renamings

US federal law required that "second-class" warships be named after US cities or towns. This ultimately included all US protected cruisers ever built. Many US protected cruisers were renamed late in their careers to clear their prestigious city names for newer, more modern cruisers under construction. They were typically given new place names, but from the state in which their original city name was located.

The USN's first three cruisers, *Atlanta*, *Boston*, and *Chicago*, were commissioned without hull numbers. The USN did not begin designating its ships with hull numbers until its fourth cruiser, *Newark*, but chose not to back-designate its first three cruisers. This meant that *Newark* received the hull designation Cruiser No. 1, which was usually (if unofficially) abbreviated to C-1. From *Newark* (built in 1891) to July 1920, all new US protected cruisers, peace cruisers, third-class cruisers, and unprotected cruisers were given the "Cruiser No. …" classification and their own unique hull number within the series begun with *Newark*; armored cruisers and scout cruisers each received their own numerical series. *San Francisco* and *Baltimore* were converted into cruiser-minelayers in 1911 and 1915 respectively.

In July 1920 the USN instituted a much more detailed classification system. Unnumbered USN ships were forced into categories and numbered; thus *Chicago* became "First Line Cruiser" CA-14. However, *Atlanta* had been disposed of in 1912, and *Boston* demilitarized into a barracks ship in 1918, meaning only *Chicago* received a hull number. The revamp of the classification system also meant many ships were renumbered to avoid duplication; thus Cruiser No. 12 (C-12) *Olympia* was redesignated as a "First Line Cruiser" in 1920, with the new hull number CA-15.

The USN overhauled its 1920 system the following year. *Chicago*, *Olympia*, *Columbia*, and *Minneapolis* were now reclassified "light cruisers" and redesignated as CL-14 through CL-17.

DESIGN AND CONSTRUCTION

The US Naval Academy had established a steam engineering curriculum in 1861, but throughout the 19th century the USN had no postgraduate school in naval architecture. So, from 1879 the USN would annually send one or two of its top Naval Academy graduates abroad to study naval shipbuilding. The preferred school was the Royal Naval College at Greenwich, England, but if no slots were available, USN students would enrol at the less prestigious *École d'Application du Genie Maritime* in Paris (a two-year course) or the University of Glasgow in Scotland (a three-year course). Only in 1901 would a USN postgraduate architecture course finally be established at the Massachusetts Institute of Technology (MIT).

Since 1842, the Navy Department had comprised parallel administrative bureaus, which Congress had intentionally decentralized to keep their posts politically weak. The resulting heavy, stagnant bureaucracy proved incompetent at providing quality ship designs in a timely manner. Therefore, on June 25, 1889, the Navy Department established the Board on Construction to rationalize US warship design. The board comprised the respective chiefs of the Bureaus of Yards & Docks; Construction & Repair; Ordnance; Equipment and Recruiting; and (after 1890) the head of naval intelligence. According to the USN's 1886 *Annual Report*:

> In the event of a conflict with a first or second class naval power, it would be quite impossible for the United States … to produce within its territory either the armor required for armored ships or the guns necessary for their armament. Nor would it be possible … to protect such articles in transit across the ocean in time of war. The country would be entirely defenseless … It is lamentable that a country like ours, with its immense products of iron and steel, should [depend] upon the manufacturers of any other nation …

The United States had historically imported more than it exported, but in 1874 it boasted a positive trade balance for the first time. By the 1880s, United States manufacturing could produce high capacities of raw industrial products, but the quality of its metallurgy lagged behind that of modern Europe. This qualitative inferiority early in the Steel Navy period held true across the fields of propulsion, armor plate, and guns.

However, Congress knew that building the new US Steel Navy at home would stimulate US industrial and technological developments. California's Senator John F. Miller said, "I am in favor of constructing American men-of-war from American material, by American workmen, to be manned by American seamen … and constructing just such ships as will be effective and useful."

During this period, the official contract price of US warships consisted of their hull and machinery, with their weapons a separate budget item supplied by the Navy Department. When contracting for ships, the USN provided the basic specifications but left the detailed plans to the shipyard. Additionally, the US

Various depictions of protected cruiser *Chicago* from an 1886 issue of *Harper's Weekly*. The basic hull and gun sponsons are highlighted, as well as views along the gun deck and bridge. Perhaps most importantly, the inclusion in *Harper's Weekly* illustrates the increasingly widespread civilian interest in the United States' new navy. (Author's collection)

An illustration of the Chester, Pennsylvania waterfront depicted in 1875, in Edward Strahan's *A Century After: Picturesque Glimpses of Philadelphia and Pennsylvania.* The view is largely of John Roach's Delaware River Iron Ship Building and Engine Works in Chester. Roach's yard was the largest and most successful American shipyard at the time when it took on the construction of the US Navy's ABCD ships. (Author's collection)

government insisted that its construction contracts for armor and guns be within 25 percent of the cost of similar articles built in Europe. This reflected the increased labor costs in the United States, but it did not include the $2.5 million capital outlay for the new manufacturing plants required.

Only three shipyards (all civilian) built the USN's protected cruisers. The USN's very first steel warships were built by John Roach's Delaware River Iron Ship Building and Engine Works, located in Chester, Pennsylvania and better known as John Roach & Sons. These included *Atlanta*, *Boston*, and *Chicago*, the first three US protected cruisers. However, in 1885 Roach was permanently driven out of the warship construction business by the overbearing political tactics of the Cleveland administration.

After Roach's government-assisted exit, all remaining US protected cruisers on the East Coast were built by Roach's primary rival, William Cramp & Sons Shipbuilding Company, just a few miles from Roach in Philadelphia, Pennsylvania. With Roach out of the way, Cramp easily became the greatest shipbuilder of the USN's Steel Navy era.

Finally, West Coast protected cruisers were built by a single shipyard, the Union Iron Works in San Francisco, California. Union Iron Works was considerably less developed than and not as efficient as the two East Coast shipyards; its government contracts were largely intended to bolster West Coast infrastructure.

US warships increasingly used electricity to power auxiliary machinery. The ABC cruisers were fitted with state-of-the-art electric lighting while still under construction. In 1891 the USN experimented with internal telephones aboard protected cruiser *Philadelphia*. Between 1899 and 1902 the USN conducted at-sea wireless telegraphy experiments, and by 1903 seven US warships had been equipped with wireless, including *Olympia*.

Propulsion

Many post-Civil War USN officers were loath to fully abandon sails for steam. Part of this was emotional, and exemplified a clash of generational values between older, traditional sailing officers

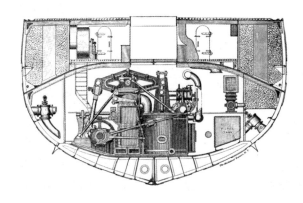

A cross-section of USS *Chicago*'s antiquated machinery. *Chicago* was driven by the highly primitive compound overhead (beam) engine, an embarrassingly archaic and un-military power plant, typically used for paddlewheels and sawmills. This design was virtually unheard of outside of the United States. (Author's collection)

and younger, more scientifically trained officers who embraced technology. There was also a belief that sailing rigging damaged in battle would collapse and foul a steamship's screws.

However, there were good reasons for not embracing steam-only propulsion in this period. Early steam power plants were inefficient and mechanically unreliable. In the 1870s, Admiral David Dixon Porter, who was essentially the acting Secretary of the Navy, argued that USN warships would need sail simply to get home during a war, as any friendly coaling stations would quickly be cut off by Britain, the presumed opponent. Porter is a controversial character in American Steel Navy histories, in which he is often portrayed as a knee-jerk reactionary. However, Porter's grasp of the emerging technological revolution was more complex. In contrast to his usual depiction, by the late 1880s, Porter was urging the use of new water-tube boilers to produce cruisers capable of exceeding 20kts, arguing that 16kt cruisers would be too slow either to run away or to catch anything worthwhile. Despite this, Porter still believed American warships should be built with sails, as contemporary European navies had not yet abandoned them.

In the early 1880s the United States trailed most advanced European nations in naval propulsion; US manufacturers could only produce power plants capable of 2.5ihp per ton, whereas European designs made at least 10ihp per ton. *Atlanta*, *Boston*, *Chicago*, and *Charleston* were powered by compound (or double-expansion) steam engines. Steam from the boilers drove the high-pressure piston, then the partially spent exhaust steam was routed to two low-pressure cylinders to extract further power. The remaining four second-generation cruisers were powered by more advanced horizontal triple expansion engines, which extracted power from the same steam three times instead of merely twice, as in a compound (or double-expansion) engine. Finally, the large and fast *Olympia*, *Columbia*, and *Minneapolis* were powered by vertical triple expansion (VTE) engines, the pinnacle of naval steam propulsion types until the introduction of the marine turbine in about 1900.

Protection

The 1886 legislation that authorized *Baltimore* included an additional $4.1 million, part of which was directed "to the manufacture or purchase of such tools and machinery or the erection of such structures as may be required for use in the manufacture of such armament ..."

Bethlehem Iron founder Joseph Wharton was insistent that American naval steel be superior to its European counterparts, regardless of expense. Wharton observed: "If by paying double the cost that Europeans pay you could get your guns or plates ten percent better than Europeans get, you could better afford to do that than to get guns or plates ten percent worse at half cost."

In addition to the definitive protective deck, by the 1880s it was acknowledged that small rapid-firing guns could do considerable damage to unbelted cruisers at short range, and bulwarks and shields were provided to defend crews on

An interior view of one of protected cruiser *Newark*'s engine rooms. A bewildering jungle of pistons, valves, connecting rods, and plumbing is apparent. This photograph was taken around 1901 by the Detroit Publishing Company. (LOC det.4a13970)

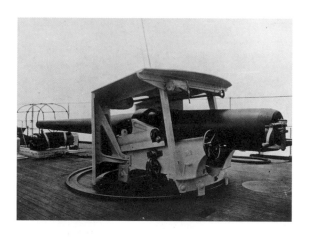

Columbia's single stern-mounted 8in./40 gun. A last-minute modification during construction, it appears the 8in. gun was intended to deter pursuing vessels. Columbia was very unusual in that the most powerful armament was stern facing. (NHHC NH 55579)

deck and behind guns. Armor plate for the first eight cruisers was all mild steel or compound, but *Olympia* included the slightly tougher nickel-steel as standard armor, while mounting the outstanding Harvey plate in the most critical places. *Columbia* and *Minneapolis* almost certainly followed this scheme as well.

Weapons

The immediate post-Civil War US Navy still clung to cast-iron smoothbore guns, even as European navies adopted breech-loading steel-constructed rifles that American industry was unable to manufacture. However, by the late 1870s, the USN's chief of ordnance, William N. Jeffers, began encouraging several American mills to develop modern, native-built US weapons.

Ultimately, both Congress and the USN would insist on developing a native ordnance industry rather than relying on imports. By 1880, Midvale Steel could produce steel forgings suitable for 6in. guns. However, *Atlanta*'s, *Boston*'s, and *Chicago*'s 8in. guns had to be ordered from English steel mills and were delivered late. Nevertheless, by 1887 the USN had begun construction of the Washington Navy Yard's Naval Gun Factory, which would contract with domestic mills to supply raw gun forgings that the government factory would then refine into finished weapons.

However, by 1892, French and British industry could produce 6in. "rapid-firing" (RF) guns. Instead of using powder bags, rapid-firing guns used brass shell casings, which greatly improved firing rates to up to 8–10 rounds per minute. Because US manufacturing lagged several years behind, contemporary US rapid-firing guns were smaller. By 1896, US industry became capable of producing 6in. RF guns, which could replace older slow-firing 6in. guns during cruiser overhauls.

Not only were rapid-firing guns more effective against torpedo attacks, but even smaller rapid-firing guns put out a considerably larger total volume of fire than bag-loaded guns. When US protected cruisers underwent refits, the USN typically replaced any remaining bag-loading batteries with the largest rapid-firing guns then available. Moreover, as more advanced powder improved muzzle velocity, existing rapid-firing guns were often replaced by new guns of the same caliber, but with longer barrels that greatly increased range, power, and accuracy.

Additionally, the three largest and newest US protected cruisers, *Olympia*, *Columbia*, and *Minneapolis*, were commissioned with torpedo tubes. The five "second-generation" cruisers that preceded them were built with openings for torpedo tubes, but none was ever fitted.

THE ABC CRUISERS 1886–89

The ABCD ships approved by the March 3, 1883 legislation had been outlined in general by the Shufeldt Board, but plans for the detailed designs had to be split between the Navy Department's various decentralized bureaus, causing delays. The USN opened construction bids on May 2, 1883. Eight different shipyards bid on the four ships. Roach had the most advanced and integrated shipyard and gave the lowest bid on all four warships. On July 3, 1883, the USN awarded Roach, a notorious Republican crony, all four contracts.

In November 1884, Democratic candidate Grover Cleveland won the US presidency. The election ended 24 years of Republican dominance – a period often rampant with severe corruption. The new Democratic administration predictably commenced vengeful "reforms." President Cleveland named William C. Whitney his new Secretary of the Navy, and Whitney's first target was Roach.

Finding minor faults with (and a broken shaft on) *Dolphin*, Whitney refused to accept the ship. He arrogantly declared all four ABCD contracts "valid but forfeit" and seized the incomplete vessels, planning to finish them in Navy yards. However, Whitney discovered the government's own dilapidated yards could not remotely handle the job, and an increasingly embarrassed Whitney was forced to take over Roach's yard entirely and finish the ships at their original locations. The government takeover ultimately forced Roach into receivership.

Sisterships USS *Boston* and USS *Atlanta* are viewed alongside each other, c.1889. The black-painted hull of *Atlanta* appears to establish this photograph as early in the Squadron of Evolution period. *Atlanta* and *Boston* were not exceptional cruisers even for their time, but they did much to establish the modern US Steel Navy. (NHHC NH 69173)

Until the ABC cruisers, the USN's newest warships were the 1,100-ton iron-hulled sloops *Alert*, *Huron*, and *Ranger*, commissioned in the mid 1870s. The new ABC cruisers were each several times larger, built of steel, and employed watertight compartments, double bottoms, state-of-the-art auxiliary machinery, internal electric lighting, and steel breech-loading guns. However, they also retained sailing rigs and could make headway without their steam propulsion engaged. In the fashion of *Esmeralda*, their protected decks were partial, shielding only machinery. In 1884 Whitney described the ABC cruisers still under construction as: "of moderate size and cost, well-protected and heavily-armed – useful and important parts of a modern naval force."

The following year, Whitney admitted that the ABC cruisers "will certainly ... be an improvement upon the previous work of the [Navy], but it is not profitable to consider them as standards of excellence for future work, nor was it to be expected that they would be."

These three cruisers and their dispatch vessel cousin, *Dolphin*, are generally regarded as a vital but intermediate step between the USN's old dilapidated wooden ships and the truly modern steel warships that would arrive by the turn of the century. The ABCD ships were assessed by modern naval historian Norman Friedman as: "Obsolescent when built, they were always more significant for their effect on the navy and its industrial base than for their direct contribution to U.S. sea power."

Atlanta class (1886)

Assistant Naval Constructor Francis T. Bowles was chiefly responsible for the design of the Atlanta class. Bowles had recently returned from Greenwich, England, where he had trained in naval architecture. His Atlanta class unsurprisingly resembled Armstrong's "Elswick" cruisers in many respects.

The designs for the Atlanta class were complete before Chile's *Esmeralda* was commissioned, but it was impossible not to compare the two schemes. They were virtually identical in dimensions, being 270ft long, and 42ft in beam, and displacing roughly 3,000 tons. Both lacked topgallant forecastles and poop decks, while *Esmeralda*'s 11ft freeboard was 1ft higher than *Atlanta*'s. However, although *Esmeralda* carried less sail than *Atlanta*, the former employed twin screws. *Esmeralda* was also more heavily armed, but *Atlanta*'s gun arrangement was superior.

The revolutionary Atlanta class naturally drew controversy before it was completed. Many USN officers considered the Atlantas' sailing rigs too decreased in size and power compared to previous USN warships, although they were more extensive than on comparable European cruisers. The Atlantas mounted two 8in./30 and six 6in./30 rifles, with one 8in./30 echeloned to port forward and one to starboard aft, allowing 8in. axial fire in both directions. However, this meant omitting the forecastle and poop decks, cutting down on freeboard and reducing seakeeping qualities, all of which had been recommendations of the original 1881 Hunt Board. The blast interference between the 6in. guns amidships and the 8in. guns at the ends was also unacceptably high by European standards.

The crew of USS *Atlanta* man the yards during the salute to the Queen of Hawai'i, May 1887. (NHHC NH 61914)

 A

THE ABC CRUISERS USS *ATLANTA* AND USS *CHICAGO*

1. *Atlanta*, the very first US protected cruiser, as seen in 1892. *Atlanta* was the first true US warship built out of steel. This steel was of a surprisingly high quality. The Schufeldt Board had insisted on an average steel ductility rate of 25 percent, with 23 percent the absolute minimum. This standard well exceeded the 20 percent average required by the British Admiralty, Lloyds Insurance Registry, and Liverpool Underwriters. After the inexperienced American steel industry balked at such unrealistic standards, Navy Secretary Chandler agreed on a compromise of 21 percent.

At the October 4, 1884 launch, *Atlanta* had been sponsored by the eight-year-old Jessie Harlan Lincoln, daughter of Secretary of War Robert Todd Lincoln and granddaughter of the late President Abraham Lincoln. *Atlanta* would spend the next 12 months being fitted out before being assigned to the North Atlantic Squadron in July 1887.

Atlanta was laid up at the New York Naval Yard in September 1895. The cruiser would be out of commission for the next five years, notably missing the 1898 Spanish–American War.

2. *Chicago* as seen in 1892, wearing an all-white hull, as well as ocher funnels, in what would become the USN's standard livery for the next 17 years. The reason for the changeover from black hulls to white was apparently simple – extended cruising in tropical climates with black-painted hulls was hot. Living conditions could be made more tolerable using white paint, which reflected the sunshine better and kept the ship cooler. This white-heavy paint scheme would likely be all but forgotten today, if it hadn't been immortalized in 1907–09 by the cruise of the Great White Fleet.

At 0513hrs, April 18, 1906, a magnitude 7.9 earthquake struck San Francisco. By 1005hrs, *Chicago*, then in San Diego, received press reports over the wireless of the San Francisco earthquake and subsequent fire that would ultimately kill 3,000 people. *Chicago* immediately raised steam and made for San Francisco, 500nm away. By 1800hrs, April 19, *Chicago* had arrived in San Francisco Bay and had moored at the base of Van Ness Avenue, which was being ravaged by fire. Beginning the following day, April 20, two officers and 19 enlisted men of *Chicago* began supervising the evacuation of 20,000 civilian refugees to the town of Tiburon across San Francisco Bay.

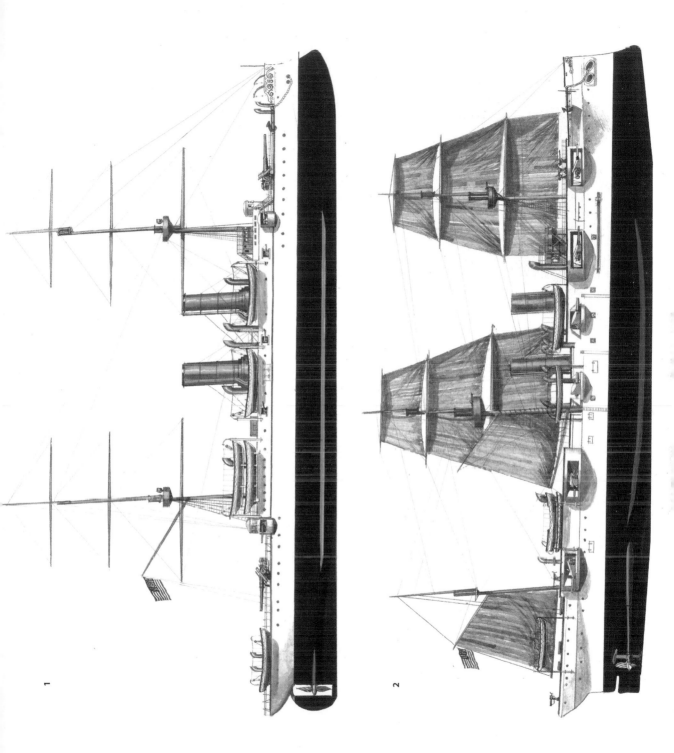

The Atlanta class was only lightly protected. The cruisers were fitted with a partial protected deck of 1.5in. that extended only 100ft – over their engines and boilers only. The conning tower and gun shields were protected by 2in. of armor.

The Atlantas' power plants were derived from the USN's recent wooden steamers. The resulting single shaft produced an asymmetric force that demanded constant rudder to keep the Atlantas underway in a straight line. This was undesirable for coordinated formation work requiring exact maneuvering, and reflects that these warships were still designed for individual cruising, rather than functioning in a battle line.

Atlanta was commissioned on July 19, 1886 and followed by *Boston* on May 2, 1887, with both ships being built at Roach's Chester, Pennsylvania yard.

Atlanta-class specifications (1886)	
Length	270ft, 3in.
Beam	42ft
Draft	7ft
Displacement	3,189 tons
Steam propulsion	single-screw, horizontal compound
Speed	15.6kts at 4,030ihp
Range	3,390nm at 10kts
Coal capacity	491 tons (480 tons *Boston*)
Auxiliary sail rig	brig; 10,400 sq ft of sail
Armament	two 8in./30 BL rifles
	six 6in./30 BL rifles
	two 6-pdr, two 3-pdr, two 1-pdr
	two 47mm guns, two 37mm guns
Protection	slopes: 1.5in.
	flats: 1.5in.
	barbettes: 2in.

USS *Atlanta* construction						
Ship	Built at	Yard	Laid down	Launched	Commissioned	Fate
Atlanta	Chester, PA	John Roach & Sons	Nov/08/1883	Oct/09/1884	Jul/19/1886	Stricken Apr/24/1912
Boston	Chester, PA	John Roach & Sons	Nov/15/1883	Dec/04/1884	May/02/1887	Disposed at sea by scuttling Apr/08/1946

USS *Chicago* (1889)

The 4,500-ton *Chicago* was designed by the USN's (chief) Naval Constructor F.L. Fernald. Like the Atlanta class, *Chicago* was fitted with a 1.5in. protective deck centered over the ship's machinery; however the protected deck extended farther, shielding a total 136ft of *Chicago*'s amidships area. The Schufeldt Board claimed that "the limit of combined efficiency and economy is reached in the cruiser of the *Chicago* type … and it condemns any policy looking to the present construction of cruisers that shall rival in speed the fastest transatlantic steamers."

Unlike the Atlanta class, *Chicago* was large enough to mount four 8in./30 rifles on the fore and aft sponsons. This left the rig unaffected and preserved a full poop deck allowing the gun deck to be fully covered. *Chicago* was originally intended to wield 15 6in./30 guns, but upon completion mounted only eight of these weapons.

USS *Chicago* viewed at the Brooklyn Naval Yard in 1901. *Chicago* is interestingly in overall haze gray, although this would not become the US Navy's standard peacetime livery until 1909. (LOC det1994013668)

The USN board assigned *Chicago*'s power plant design to a civilian engineer, a clear mistake. Five double-ended boilers provided steam to an archaic compound overhead (or beam) engine, with the "walking beams" protruding above deck – a merchantman design and extremely vulnerable for a warship. In addition, *Chicago*'s furnaces were made of brick. The entire combination was accused of being of "doubtful design" during construction. The resulting 5,000ihp power plant propelled *Chicago* at 15kts. However, unlike the Atlanta class, *Chicago* did employ twin screws as well as a three-masted sail rig and bowsprit.

Chicago received a major overhaul during an 1895–98 decommissioning. The power plant was completely replaced with a more modern design and the funnels were lengthened for increased draft. The result was 9,000ihp and a new 18kt top speed. *Chicago*'s sailing rig and mainmast were removed, and the foremast replaced by a military mast. Additional 1–1.5in. deck plating and armor strips were added to key locations. The eight 6in./30 guns were replaced by 14 5in./40 RF guns. *Chicago* was then partially reconstructed in 1902, increasing displacement to 5,000 tons, which finally allowed for the mounting of a full protective deck.

In 1907 *Chicago* helped several other ships evacuate 20,000 refugees from the San Francisco earthquake. Between 1912 and 1917 *Chicago* served in the Pennsylvania and Massachusetts naval militias as a training ship and was fitted with an additional battery of six 4in./40 RF guns.

To clear the way for the Northampton-class heavy cruiser CA-28, *Chicago* was renamed *Alton* on July 16, 1928 and was reclassified as IX-5.

Chicago, c.1898–99, after an early modernization. This particular overhaul caused *Chicago* to miss the 1898 Spanish–American War, but it was the first of several major conversions that helped *Chicago* to have one of the longest careers of all the US protected cruisers. (LOC LC-D4-32262)

USS *Chicago* specifications (1889)	
Length	325ft
Beam	48ft, 2in.
Draft	19ft
Displacement	4,500 tons
Steam propulsion	twin-screw, compound overhead
Speed	15.3kts at 5,084ihp
Range	4,949nm at 10kts
Coal capacity	940 tons
Auxiliary sail rig	bark; 14,880 sq ft sail
Armament	four 8in./30 BL rifles
	eight 6in./30 BL rifles
	two 6-pdr, two 1-pdr
	four 47mm guns, two 37mm guns
	two .45-70 Gatling guns
Protection	slopes: 1.5in.
	flats: 1.5in.
	gun shields: 4in.
Complement	33 officers, 376 enlisted

USS *Chicago* construction						
Ship	Built at	Yard	Laid down	Launched	Commissioned	Fate
Chicago	Chester, PA	John Roach & Sons	Dec/19/1883	Dec/05/1885	Apr/17/1889	Hulk sank under tow after being sold Jul/08/1936

SECOND-GENERATION CRUISERS 1889–91

Between 1889 and 1891 the USN commissioned five additional protected cruisers. This second generation of cruisers, the first to receive hull numbers, proved categorically superior to the ABC cruisers, which were essentially experimental designs. All five new cruisers displaced at least 4,000 tons, being substantially larger than the Atlanta class, while *Baltimore* slightly exceeded *Chicago* at 4,600 tons. At 18–19kts, they were 4kts faster than the ABCD ships. They also followed contemporary European practice by mounting full rather than partial protective decks.

USS *Newark* C-1 (1891)

After authorizing the original ABC cruisers in 1883, the lame-duck Republican Congress authorized two additional protected cruisers on March 3, 1885 – its last day in office. These became *Newark* (Cruiser No. 1) and *Charleston* (Cruiser No. 2), the first USN cruisers to be assigned hull numbers.

Because Whitney had so thoroughly assailed the design and construction of the ABCD ships, anything other than complete redesigns of the newly authorized ships would have resulted in political humiliation. Whitney therefore called for a domestic design competition for *Newark*. Yet Whitney now found that the Navy Department's design capacity was embarrassingly limited, as he apparently rejected the Naval Advisory Board's submission. In September 1885, a new, Whitney-assigned American board submitted its basic design for the new US cruiser. This new design received a poop deck

Cruiser No. 1 USS *Newark* viewed in 1891 upon completion. Like most of the early US steel warships, *Newark* went through major design issues as the Navy Department struggled to bring its entire institution into the modern industrial era. (LC-DIG-det-4a14452)

and was intended as a flagship, boasting separate admiral's and captain's cabins and high freeboard for superior seakeeping.

Two horizontal triple expansion engines combined for nearly 9,000ihp, pushing *Newark* to 19kts. The original board had wished to do away with sails, but *Newark* was nevertheless completed with a full sailing rig. Apparently, some thought was given to arming *Newark* with 8in. guns in sponsons, but it was decided this would be too heavy on a 4,000-ton displacement. *Newark* was instead fitted with a heavy battery of 12 6in./30 guns.

The USN's Bureau of Construction & Repair was a full year late preparing *Newark*'s plans for bids. The subsequent bidding process then saw every bidder exceed the funds allotted, delaying construction a second year. Only in 1887 was *Newark*'s contract awarded to Philadelphia's Cramp shipyards, which finally began construction in June 1888. Although *Newark* was officially the first of the five new second-generation cruisers authorized between 1885 and 1887, the cruiser would be the last commissioned, on February 2, 1891.

USS *Newark* specifications (1891)	
Length	310ft
Beam	49ft, 2in.
Draft	18ft, 9in.
Displacement	4,083 tons
Steam propulsion	twin-screw, horizontal triple expansion
Speed	19.0kts at 8,869ihp
Range	5,656nm at 10kts
Coal capacity	400 tons
Auxiliary sail rig	bark; 11,932 sq ft sail
Armament	12 6in./30 BL rifles
	four 6-pdr, four 3-pdr
	two 1-pdr, two 37mm guns
	two .45-70 Gatling guns
Protection	slopes: 3in.
	flats: 2in.
	gun shields: 2in.
	conning tower: 3in.
Complement	34 officers, 350 enlisted

USS *Newark* (Cruiser No. 1) construction						
Ship	Built at	Yard	Laid down	Launched	Commissioned	Fate
Newark	Philadelphia, PA	William Cramp & Sons	Jun/12/1888	Mar/19/1890	Feb/02/1891	Sold Sept/07/1936

USS *Charleston* C-2 (1889)

Whitney became sceptical of American design ability after *Newark*'s troubled development. He instead looked to European sources for Cruiser No. 2 *Charleston*. From Armstrong, Whitney obtained a set of plans supposedly based on Japan's highly regarded cruiser *Naniwa*. Only later was it discovered that the purchased Armstrong plans were a sloppy amalgamation of *Naniwa*, the Italian cruisers *Etna* and *Giovanni Bausan*, and the original *Esmeralda*. *Charleston*'s contractor, Union Iron Works, would be forced to make extensive changes to *Charleston* while the cruiser was under construction.

Armstrong's plans powered *Charleston* with obsolete inclined compound (double expansion) engines, the last US cruiser fitted with this type. Their combined 6,500ihp drove the 4,040-ton cruiser to 18kts. *Charleston* was also the first US cruiser designed and commissioned without sails.

Although the original Armstrong plans had two end-mounted 10in. guns, the final American design was fitted with a pair of 8in./35 guns. *Charleston*'s secondary battery was comprised of six 6in./30 guns. Four 6-pdr, two 3-pdr, two 1-pdr, four 37mm guns, and two .45-70 Gatling guns provided rapid-fire capability.

B

SECOND-GENERATION CRUISERS *NEWARK* AND *CHARLESTON*

1. USS *Newark* (C-1). On June 25, 1892, *Newark* was made flagship of Rear Admiral A.E.K. Benham's South Atlantic Squadron. Weeks later, on July 17, *Newark* set sail for Cadiz, Spain to participate in celebrations for the 400th anniversary of Christopher Columbus' voyage that discovered the New World. *Newark* reached Cadiz on July 30, then put in at Genoa, Italy, Columbus' birthplace, on August 30. After staying several weeks, *Newark* left Genoa on August 30 and spent the next five months cruising the Mediterranean and Adriatic, calling at many ports. Finally, on February 11, 1893, the cruiser arrived at Cadiz. A week later *Newark* departed to make the return trip across the Atlantic – only this time towing a full-scale reproduction of Columbus' historic caravel *Nina*. *Newark* would spend the next several months towing the *Nina* replica to several ports in North America and across the Caribbean, before finally returning to Rio de Janeiro and more traditional South Atlantic Squadron duty on October 20, 1894.

2. USS *Charleston* (C-2). *Charleston* is seen painted overall wartime haze gray in the 1898 Spanish–American War configuration, when the cruiser famously captured Guam without a fight. *Charleston* had begun the war in California and had been ordered to Manila to reinforce Commodore George Dewey's squadron. The cruiser first stopped at Honolulu, where it was assigned to a convoy with US troop transports *City of Peking*, *City of Sydney*, and *Australia*. The four-ship convoy sortied from Honolulu to Manila on June 4, 1898. Aboard *Charleston* were sealed orders to capture Spanish-occupied Guam on the way, with the caveat that "operations should not take more than one or two days." While en route, *Charleston*'s Captain Glass drilled his crew with relentless gunnery training, as rumors were that a Spanish gunboat was stationed there.

However, when *Charleston* and the transports reached Guam on June 20, only a Japanese merchantman was present. *Charleston* entered Guam's Agana harbor and fired 14 3-pdr rounds at Guam's Fort Cruz. There was no response, and so *Charleston* anchored in a dominant position in the harbor, with the transports a half mile further out to sea. A Spanish boat then approached *Charleston*. On board was Lieutenant Garcia Gutierrez, the port commander, who apologized for not returning the salute and offered to do so if he could borrow some powder. Almost unbelievably, the Guam garrison had not received a Spanish ship in a year and a half and had never been informed Spain and the United States were at war.

Within two weeks, *Charleston* had joined Dewey's Asiatic Squadron at Manila. By August the Spanish–American War was essentially over, but it was immediately replaced by the Filipino–American War. *Charleston* operated in support of US anti-insurgency operations. However, on November 2, 1899 *Charleston* ran aground on an uncharted reef off Camiguin Island north of Luzon. Because *Charleston* was clearly wrecked beyond repair, the crew abandoned ship and set up camp at a nearby island. They then sent *Charleston*'s sailing launch for help, while moving their impromptu camp to Camiguin. Gunboat USS *Helena* would arrive to rescue *Charleston*'s men on November 12.

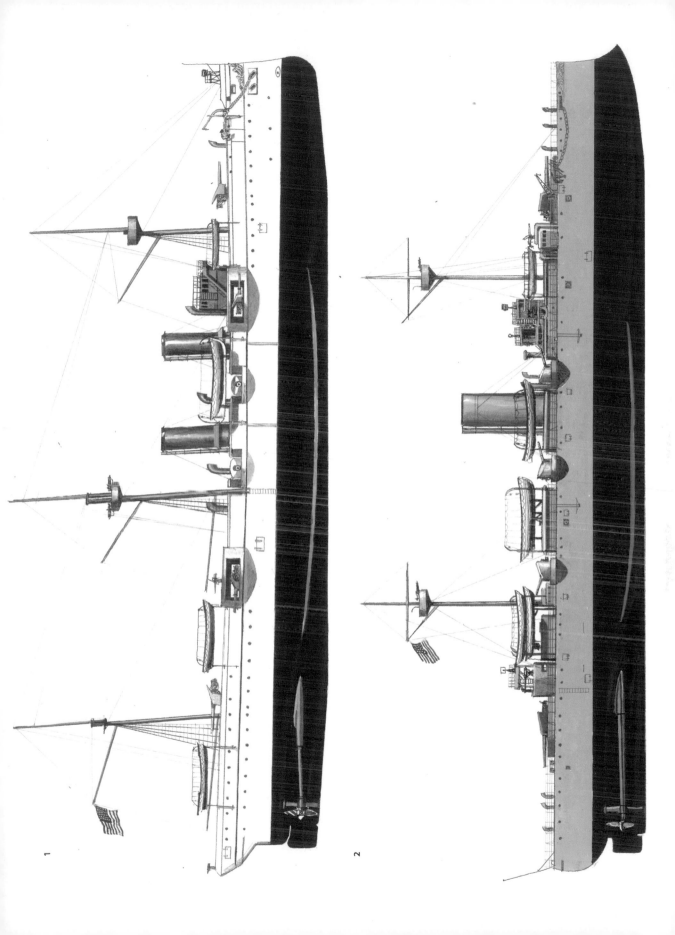

Cruiser No. 2 USS *Charleston* at Mare Island. *Charleston* has just been commissioned. The planned 8in. battery is temporarily replaced with 6in. guns until the 8in. guns can be delivered from the US East Coast via railroad. (LOC LC-DIG-det-4a14138)

Charleston was commissioned in 1889, the first of the new second-generation protected cruisers to enter service. En route to Manila, *Charleston* singlehandedly forced the surrender of Spanish-occupied Guam on June 20–21, 1898. The cruiser spent the war's final month under Commodore George Dewey, then engaged in the Filipino–American War immediately afterwards. It was in the Philippines, on November 2, 1899, that *Charleston* ran aground on an uncharted reef north of Luzon, being wrecked beyond repair and becoming the first US steel warship to be lost in active service.

USS *Charleston* specifications (1889)	
Length	312ft
Beam	46ft
Draft	19ft, 7in.
Displacement	4,040 tons
Steam propulsion	twin-screw, horizontal compound
Speed	18.2kts at 6,666ihp
Range	2,990nm at 10kts
Coal capacity	328 tons
Armament	two 8in./35 BL rifles
	six 6in./30 BL rifles
	four 6-pdr, two 3-pdr
	two 1-pdr, four 37mm guns
	two .45-70 Gatling guns
Protection	slopes: 3in.
	flats: 2in.
	gun shields: 3in.
	conning tower: 2in.
Complement	20 officers, 280 enlisted

USS *Charleston* (Cruiser No. 2) construction						
Ship	Built	Yard	Laid down	Launched	Commissioned	Fate
Charleston	San Francisco, CA	Union Iron Works	Jan/20/1887	Jul/19/1887	Dec/26/1889	Wrecked on reef off Philippines Nov/02/1899

USS *Baltimore* C-3 (1890)

Congress authorized Cruiser No. 3 on August 3, 1886. For the future *Baltimore*, Whitney also purchased Armstrong plans. These were based on Armstrong's failed bid for the Spanish cruiser *Reina Regente* and had been prepared by W.H. White, who later became Director of Naval Construction in Britain's Admiralty.

At 4,600 tons, *Baltimore* was the largest US protected cruiser yet built. *Baltimore* was intended as an evolutionary improvement to *Charleston* in

USS *Baltimore*, the sixth US protected cruiser and third to receive an official hull number. *Baltimore* was the largest of the early US protected cruisers until *Olympia*, which displaced slightly more than *Chicago*. (LOC LC-DIG-det-4a14007)

every way, being more heavily armed, better protected, and powered by more modern machinery.

Four 8in./35 guns were deployed on forecastle and poop sponsons. Mounted one level below them on the gun deck were six 6in./30 guns. An additional four 6-pdr, two 3-pdr, two 1-pdr, and four 37mm guns rounded out *Baltimore*'s battery. *Baltimore*'s protective deck was 4in. thick on the slopes and 2.5in. thick on the flats, an increase of 33 percent and 25 percent respectively over *Charleston*.

Four double-ended horizontal return tubular boilers powered a pair of horizontal triple expansion engines, the very first triple expansion type installed on a US warship. *Baltimore*'s more powerful and more efficient engines could generate 10,000ihp under forced draft, allowing nearly 20kts. A standard load of 400 tons of coal allowed a range of 3,838nm at 10kts. Like *Charleston*, *Baltimore* was built without sails.

Built at Philadelphia's Cramp yards, *Baltimore* was commissioned on January 7, 1890. *Baltimore* achieved almost immediate notoriety as the central player behind the 1891 *Baltimore* Crisis with Chile.

USS *Baltimore* specifications (1890)	
Length	327ft, 6in.
Beam	48ft, 6in.
Draft	20ft, 6in.
Displacement	4,600 tons
Steam propulsion	twin-screw, horizontal triple expansion
Speed	19.6kts at 10,064ihp
Range	3,838nm at 10kts
Coal capacity	400 tons
Armament	four 8in./35 BL rifles
	six 6in./30 BL rifles
	four 6-pdr, two 3-pdr
	two 1-pdr, four 37mm guns
Protection	slopes: 4in.
	flats: 2.5in.
	gun shields: 4.5in.
Complement	36 officers, 350 enlisted

USS *Baltimore* (Cruiser No. 3) construction						
Ship	Built at	Yard	Laid down	Launched	Commissioned	Fate
Baltimore	Philadelphia, PA	William Cramp & Sons	May/05/1887	Oct/06/1888	Jan/07/1890	Sold Feb/16/1942

Cruiser No. 4 USS *Philadelphia*, c.1892–93 mounted 12 6in. guns, as 8in. guns were too slow-firing and impractical on small cruisers. *Philadelphia* was designed by the US Navy. (LOC LC-D4-20878)

USS *Philadelphia* C-4 (1890)

Although Whitney next requested an additional four large, fast cruisers, Congress authorized only two additional protected cruisers on March 3, 1887. These became Cruiser No. 4 *Philadelphia* and Cruiser No. 5 *San Francisco*. *Philadelphia* copied *Baltimore*'s Elswick-designed hull, with a full battery of 12 6in./30 guns mounted on the forecastle and poop deck replacing the 8in./35 battery and fore and aft sponsons. Remaining weaponry comprised four 6-pdr, four 3-pdr, two 1-pdr, and three 37mm guns.

Philadelphia and the later *San Francisco* were contractually required to reach at least 19kts. To accomplish this, *Philadelphia* was powered by two horizontal triple expansion engines designed to reach 10,500ihp. These were fed by an odd assortment of four Scotch double-ended boilers, one Scotch single-ended boiler, and locomotive (or "fire-tube") boilers. Although *Philadelphia*'s power plant only made 8,814ihp on trials, this proved enough to reach 19.7kts.

C **SECOND-GENERATION CRUISERS *PHILADELPHIA* AND *SAN FRANCISCO***

1. USS *Philadelphia* (C-4). *Philadelphia* is seen as the cruiser appeared in July 1898, when recommissioned to represent the USN at the ceremonies transferring the Republic of Hawai'i to the United States.

Immediately after commissioning, *Philadelphia* was designated flagship of the North American Squadron on August 18, 1890. In March 1893, the cruiser was assigned as flagship of the temporary Naval Review Fleet at Hampton Roads. Then on April 24, *Philadelphia* led a combined American and international flotilla north to New York, where additional foreign ships were waiting that swelled the international fleet to 35 warships. President Cleveland reviewed the fleet on April 27. After several days of celebrations and parades ashore, the review was broken up on April 30.

Philadelphia was subsequently transferred to the Pacific, where upon arrival in San Francisco on August 22, 1893 the cruiser became the flagship of the Pacific station. After touring various North American, South American, and Hawai'ian ports, *Philadelphia* was laid up at the Mare Island Navy Yard on December 18, 1897. *Philadelphia* was then recommissioned as Pacific station flagship on July 9, 1898. The cruiser steamed from San Francisco and arrived at Honolulu on August 3. Nine days later, on August 12, *Philadelphia* and US steam sloop-of-war *Mohican* put armed parties ashore participating in the formal annexation handover of Hawai'i to the United States.

2. USS *San Francisco* (C-5). *San Francisco* is viewed in 1902, during the cruiser's second assignment to the European Squadron. The cruiser is wearing the USN's usual white and ocher peacetime livery from the period, which the USN ultimately retired fleet-wide in 1909.

San Francisco was converted to a cruiser-minelayer in 1910 and recommissioned in reserve status in 1911. After the United States' entry into World War I, *San Francisco* was eventually assigned to the US Mine Force tasked to deploy the massive North Sea Mine Barrage. This force was divided into two squadrons, and on April 10, 1918, *San Francisco* was named flagship of Captain Reginald Belknap's Mine Squadron 1, comprising *San Francisco*, converted freighters *Housatonic*, *Canonicus*, and *Canandaigua*, and fleet tug *Quinnebaug*. They would operate out of Inverness and Invergordon, Scotland.

After considerable training and preparation, *San Francisco* and Mine Squadron 1 executed their first minelaying mission on June 8, 1918, successfully laying 153 mines. Although dogged throughout with technical problems, the squadron continued to increase its efficiency. On September 20, the ninth mine-laying expedition by Mine Squadron 1 laid 5,520 mines in three hours and 50 minutes, the single-mission record for the North Sea mining campaign. This was despite being stalked from the harbor by a U-boat, which was attacked several times by the squadron's escorting destroyers. Mining Squadron 1 executed its final minelaying mission on October 26, 1918, laying another 3,760 mines. With the war's end seemingly days away, further missions were suspended.

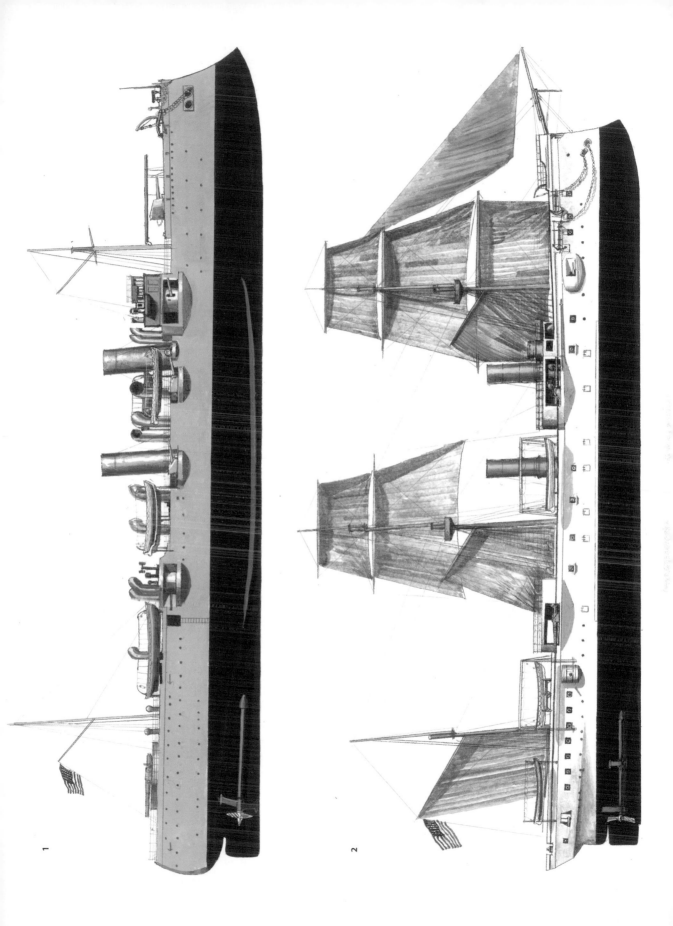

Built by Philadelphia's Cramp yards, *Philadelphia* was commissioned on July 28, 1890. In 1898 *Philadelphia*'s 6in./30 guns were converted to rapid firing. However, in 1904 *Philadelphia* was converted into a training ship, and all guns were removed. In November 1912, *Philadelphia* was turned into a prison ship, before being changed back into a receiving ship in January 1916. In July 1920 *Philadelphia* received the hull designator IX-24 before finally being struck in 1926.

USS *Philadelphia* specifications (1890)	
Length	327ft, 6in.
Beam	48ft, 6in.
Draft	19ft, 2in.
Displacement	4,324 tons
Steam propulsion	twin-screw, horizontal triple expansion
Speed	19.7kts at 8,814ihp
Range	6,354nm at 10kts
Coal capacity	525 tons
Armament	12 6in./30 BL rifles
	four 6-pdr, four 3-pdr
	two 1-pdr, three 37mm guns
Protection:	slopes: 4in.
	flats: 2.5in.
Complement	34 officers, 350 enlisted

USS *Philadelphia* (Cruiser No. 4) construction						
Ship	Built at	Yard	Laid down	Launched	Commissioned	Fate
Philadelphia	Philadelphia, PA	William Cramp & Sons	Mar/22/1888	Sep/07/1889	Jul/28/1890	Stricken Nov/24/1926

USS *San Francisco* C-5 (1890)

Neither *Baltimore* nor *Newark* had been completed by 1887, meaning it was still unclear which design might be superior. The USN apparently hedged its bets, dividing its 1887 cruiser pair between the two earlier designs. The 4,083-ton *San Francisco* was therefore based on *Newark*'s hull. Two horizontal triple expansion engines produced 9,913ihp for a top speed of 19.5kts.

Like *Newark*, *San Francisco*'s main battery comprised 12 6in./30 guns. However, only eight were mounted in broadside sponsons. The remaining four 6in./30 guns were deployed one deck higher, with two in the bow and two in the stern. Four 6-pdr, four 3-pdr, two 1-pdr, and four 37mm guns rounded out *San Francisco*'s battery. In 1902 the 6in./30 battery was replaced by more powerful 6in./40 weapons.

Built at Union Ironworks, *San Francisco* was commissioned in 1890 under Captain William T. Sampson, who would officially command the US North Atlantic Squadron at the blockade of Santiago in 1898.

Between 1908 and 1911, *San Francisco* was converted into a cruiser-minelayer. In this guise the cruiser was rearmed with eight 5in./40 guns, and reboilered with eight Babcock & Wilcox boilers. By the time of *San Francisco*'s participation in the 1918 Northern Mine barrage, the cruiser's armament had been reduced to four 5in./51 guns.

Cruiser No. 5 USS *San Francisco* fully dressed. The cruiser is rather interestingly flying the Italian ensign. This photograph was likely taken during *San Francisco*'s service with the European Squadron in 1895–96. (LOC det.4a14708)

In accordance with *San Francisco*'s minelaying mission, the cruiser was redesignated CM-2 on July 17, 1920. On January 1, 1931 *San Francisco* was renamed *Yosemite* to clear that name for CA-38, a New Orleans-class heavy cruiser commissioned in 1934.

USS *San Francisco* specifications (1890)	
Length	310ft
Beam	49ft, 2in.
Draft	18ft, 9in.
Displacement	4,083 tons
Steam propulsion	twin-screw, horizontal triple expansion
Speed	19.5kts at 9,913ihp
Range	3,432nm at 10kts
Coal capacity	350 tons
Auxiliary sail rig	three-masted schooner
Armament	12 6in./30 BL rifles
	four 6-pdr, four 3-pdr
	two 1-pdr, four 37mm guns
Protection	slopes: 3in.
	flats: 2in.
	conning tower: 3in.
Complement	34 officers, 350 enlisted
Cost	$1.43 million

USS *San Francisco* (Cruiser No. 5) construction						
Ship	Built at	Yard	Laid down	Launched	Commissioned	Fate
San Francisco	San Francisco, CA	Union Iron Works	Aug/14/1888	Oct/26/1889	Nov/15/1890	Stricken Jun/08/1937

FAST CRUISERS 1894–95

By the late 1880s, Whitney was convinced that existing US cruisers were too slow, and he helped inaugurate a brief but intense institutional fad in the USN for high speed. Between 1888 and 1891, Congress would authorize three unusually large and swift new protected cruisers, resulting in the unique *Olympia* and the subsequent two-ship Columbia class (*Columbia* and *Minneapolis*). Although all three were designed as fast commerce destroyers, *Olympia* proved to be a well-balanced scheme providing good firepower, speed, and protection, qualities which insured *Olympia* a relatively long and active career.

However, the subsequent *Columbia* design took the fast but balanced *Olympia* concept to an illogical extreme. Indeed, *Columbia* and *Minneapolis* proved too specialized for high speed, being too lightly armed to be consistently useful and so expensive to operate that they would spend most of their careers laid up in reserve. Within a year of *Columbia*'s commissioning an influential USN officer would declare that "The craze for speed is the curse of naval architecture." Responding to the sudden and widespread criticism, the USN's naval engineering chief George Melville rued that he had been asked to design a fast ship, "and now we have beaten our foreign friends, and we are told that fast ships are useless."

USS *Olympia* C-6 (1895)

On September 7, 1888, Congress authorized seven new cruisers comprising four different types. One of these, Cruiser No. 6, was a unique design that was expected to reach 20kts and cost no more than $1.8 million. The resulting 5,870-ton *Olympia* would prove notably larger, more powerful, and several knots faster than any previous US protected cruiser.

As the only bidder, San Francisco's Union Iron Works was duly awarded the *Olympia* contract. It received 102 pages of required USN specifications as well as 12 plans. Certain heavy castings and forgings were provided by the nearby Pacific Rolling Mills, while Pittsburgh's Carnegie Steel supplied boilerplate. *Olympia*'s armor was contracted to Bethlehem Steel, but after Bethlehem's deliveries fell behind, Bethlehem's rival Carnegie supplied the rest. In both cases, the armor plate was manufactured in Pennsylvania and shipped to San Francisco by railroad. Because *Olympia* was intended as the Asiatic station flagship, the cruiser would be fitted out with an admiral's cabin.

By late 1890, new Navy Secretary Benjamin Tracy would claim that *Olympia*'s "sustained speed, exceptional coal endurance, powerful battery, and a certain amount of armor protection make her a cruiser of no ordinary character." *Olympia*'s unusual size, Tracy continued, would allow "an increase in endurance

USS *Columbia* running trials in 1893. *Columbia* proved extremely fast, as the cruiser had been designed. However, trials were always performed with a brand-new ship in ideal conditions, with the shipyard naturally inclined to do whatever possible to meet contractual requirements. (NHHC NH 55288)

D **THE FAST CRUISERS**

1. USS *Olympia* (C-6). *Olympia* was easily the best-designed, most powerful, and ultimately most celebrated protected cruiser the USN ever built. *Olympia* is seen in 1895 shortly after commissioning with sail rig deployed.

Although an excellent design, *Olympia* likely would have lived out a career in obscurity, but fate had other ideas. *Olympia* was to be Commodore George Dewey's flagship at the May 1, 1898 Battle of Manila Bay. The crushing US victory, Dewey's memorable and quotable *sangfroid*, and *Olympia*'s own key role in the battle all combined to make the cruiser the enduring symbol of the American Steel Navy.

However, by 1954 Congress had declared that it would dispose of all obsolete historical ships in USN custody except for the sailing frigate *Constitution*. The USN requested $650,000 "in ready cash to restore and make a public memorial of the warship *Olympia*." A group called Committee to Save the Olympia was established to try and save *Olympia* and preserve the cruiser as a Philadelphia waterfront attraction. The Committee was required to raise $250,000 for initial repairs before the USN would even transfer the ship, a process which took several years. On September 11, 1957, the USN officially handed *Olympia* over to the committee, which was now called the Cruiser Olympia Association. *Olympia* was officially reopened to the public on October 6, 1958.

2. USS *Minneapolis* (C-13). Columbia-class cruiser *Minneapolis* appears as seen in 1898, with the hull painted a wartime haze gray. *Minneapolis* was the first US warship named after Minnesota's largest city. Although Maine's Bath Iron Works had submitted the lowest bid to build *Minneapolis*, it was rejected, as the USN did not believe Bath could manufacture *Minneapolis*' engines, nor complete the cruiser on time. Cramp, the only yard that had bid on *Columbia*, lowered its *Minneapolis* bid by $55,000 to match Bath and was accordingly awarded the contract.

During the 1894 builder's trials, *Minneapolis* reached 23kts, earning a $414,000 bonus for Cramp. *Minneapolis* was commissioned at Philadelphia on December 13, 1894. First assigned to the North Atlantic Squadron, the cruiser was transferred to the European Squadron in December 1895. As flagship, *Minneapolis* visited Kronstadt (St Petersburg), Russia, between May 13 and June 19, 1897, to pay American tribute to the coronation of Tsar Nicholas II. Immediately after coming home, on July 7, 1897, *Minneapolis* was placed in reserve at Philadelphia, barely 18 months after being first commissioned.

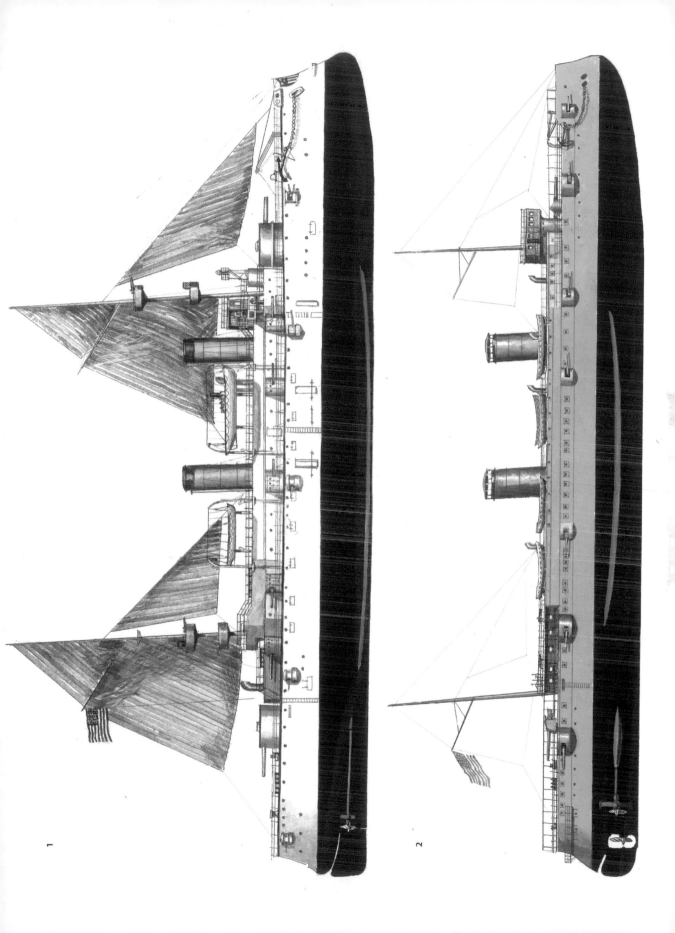

The view from atop *Olympia*'s conning tower, in August 2022, standing where Commodore Dewey stood during the Battle of Manila Bay, May 1, 1898. Directly beneath Dewey was *Olympia*'s Captain Gridley in the armored conning tower. (Author)

and sustained speed." To increase *Olympia*'s fireroom space, Union Iron Works lengthened *Olympia* by 10ft at its own expense. Six Scotch boilers provided steam to two VTE engines. Their combined 17,313ihp drove *Olympia* at nearly 22kts.

For a medium-sized protected cruiser of the era, *Olympia* was well armored, with a full protective deck that was 2in. thick on the flats and almost 5in. thick on the slopes. The 8in. turrets were protected by 3.5in. of Harvey steel, while the barbettes were armored with 4.5in. of nickel-steel.

For the primary battery, *Olympia* mounted four 8-in./35 BL guns in twin turrets fore-and-aft. *Olympia* was the only US protected cruiser to employ turrets for its 8in. battery. *Olympia* additionally mounted a powerful secondary armament of ten 5in./40 rapid-firing guns, along with 14 6-pdr, six 1-pdr, and four Gatling guns. *Olympia* was equipped with six torpedo tubes for the 18in. Whitehead Mark 1, which had a range of 800yds at 26.5kts. However, *Olympia*'s torpedo tubes were removed in 1900, while the 8in. gun turrets were landed in 1916.

Olympia was commissioned on February 5, 1895. Although not the final protected cruiser authorized, *Olympia* was the last protected cruiser commissioned by the United States. On May 1, 1898, *Olympia* led the US Asiatic Squadron into Manila Bay as Commodore George Dewey's flagship. The crushing US victory that followed ensured *Olympia*'s place in history.

USS *Olympia* specifications (1895)	
Length	340ft
Beam	53ft, 1in.
Draft	21ft, 6in.
Displacement	5,870 tons
Steam propulsion	twin-screw, vertical triple expansion (VTE)
Speed	21.7kts at 17,313ihp
Range	6,105nm at 10kts
Coal capacity	1,150 tons
Auxiliary sail rig	two-masted schooner
Armament	four 8in./35 BL rifles
	ten 5in./40 RF guns
	14 6-pdr, six 1-pdr
	four .45-70 Gatling guns
	six 18in. torpedo tubes
Protection	slopes: 4.75in.
	flats: 2in.
Complement	33 officers, 395 enlisted

USS *Olympia* (Cruiser No. 6) construction						
Ship	Built at	Yard	Laid down	Launched	Commissioned	Fate
Olympia	San Francisco, CA	Union Iron Works	Jun/17/1891	Nov/05/1892	Feb/05/1895	Currently museum ship in Philadelphia

Columbia class (1894)

Congress authorized Cruiser No. 12 on June 30, 1890. A highly specialized commerce raider, the future *Columbia* was designed specifically to run down and destroy hostile (i.e., British) auxiliary cruisers converted from large and fast transatlantic passenger liners.

At 412ft end to end, *Columbia* was the USN's longest warship upon commissioning, while a 7,375-ton displacement produced the heaviest US protected cruiser ever built. Reaching the design speed of 22kts demanded an unprecedented 21,000ihp. Such power required three VTEs driving three shafts, a design first for the USN. *Columbia*'s two outer VTEs could be disengaged for increased fuel efficiency, allowing the cruiser to reach 15kts on one-third power or 20kts at two-thirds power.

Columbia was initially designed with four 6in./40 guns, with one pair each fore and aft. However, the after 6in./40 pair was ultimately replaced by a single centerline-mounted 8in./40 rifle, which *Columbia*'s designers apparently intended to deter pursuit by more powerful cruisers. This change was made in 1891, when *Columbia* was already under construction. In addition to the after 8in./40 gun and two bow-mounted 6in./40 RF guns, *Columbia* carried eight 4in./40 RF guns, 12 6-pdr, four 1-pdr, and four Gatling guns. Four 14in. Howell torpedo tubes were also mounted.

Columbia's protected deck was the standard 4in. thick on the slopes and 2.5in. on the flats. Therefore, despite *Columbia* being 60–70 percent larger than *Philadelphia* and *Baltimore*, the cruiser's protective scheme was identical. However, *Columbia* likely deployed a combination of more efficient nickel-steel and Harvey armor like *Olympia*. Additionally, *Columbia*'s three VTEs were each located in self-contained engine rooms, while *Columbia*'s centerline shaft was 15ft astern of the outboard shafts; all these design elements would conceivably localize potential damage.

Congress authorized a second Columbia-class cruiser on March 2, 1891, which became *Minneapolis* (Cruiser No. 13). Both *Columbia* and *Minneapolis* would be built at Philadelphia's Cramp yards. *Columbia* was commissioned on April 23, 1894, followed by *Minneapolis* on December 13, 1894. However, Whitney's emphasis on higher speed proved the swansong for a USN commerce raiding doctrine. By the early 1890s, USN naval doctrine had swung decisively towards a battle fleet strategy. The Columbias were therefore the last US cruisers (indeed, arguably the last US warships) designed specifically as commerce destroyers.

Although *Columbia* and *Minneapolis* were sisterships, their silhouettes differed remarkably. Instead of the original design of three funnels, *Columbia* was built with four slim funnels, while *Minneapolis* was completed with two wider funnels. In true pirate fashion, the cruisers' differing silhouettes were apparently designed to mimic specific transatlantic liners. Whether such a dubious ruse would have worked was never tested.

A designed coal capacity of 2,135 tons was expected to give the Columbia class an eye-watering range of 25,520nm at 10kts, allowing them to circumnavigate the planet without refueling. The USN's 1890 *Annual Report* claimed that six Columbia class cruisers "would exterminate the commerce of any country [and therefore] preclude an attack from a commercial state, however threatening its demands,

An 1899 view of *Columbia*'s stern, including the officers' stern walk, a rare feature on US warships. This was the theoretical view *Columbia* was designed to show more powerful enemies, a dubious and short-lived USN strategy. (LOC-LC-DIG-det-4a14185)

E

USS *COLUMBIA* (C-12)

"Columbia" is the poetic name for the United States, given the nation's feminine personification. Although there is a city or town named Columbia in most US states, Cruiser No. 12 was specifically named for the capital of South Carolina. First commissioned on April 23, 1894, *Columbia* is seen in the 1896 configuration.

Columbia was nicknamed "The Pirate" by shipyard workers and "The Gem of the Ocean" by an overenthusiastic press. During Cramp's November 18, 1893 speed trials, *Columbia* reached 25.31kts over a 7.74nm stretch, setting a new world record. Returning from Europe in summer 1895, *Columbia* set a transatlantic record (Southampton, England to Sandy Hook, New Jersey) of six days, 23hrs, and 49mins and an average speed of 18.41kts, knocking 16hrs and 35mins off the previous record set by American Lines steamship *New York*.

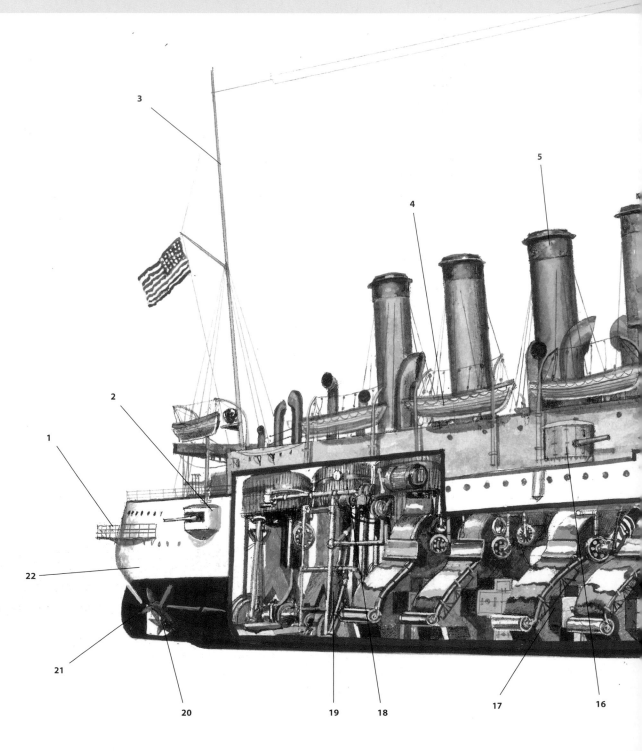

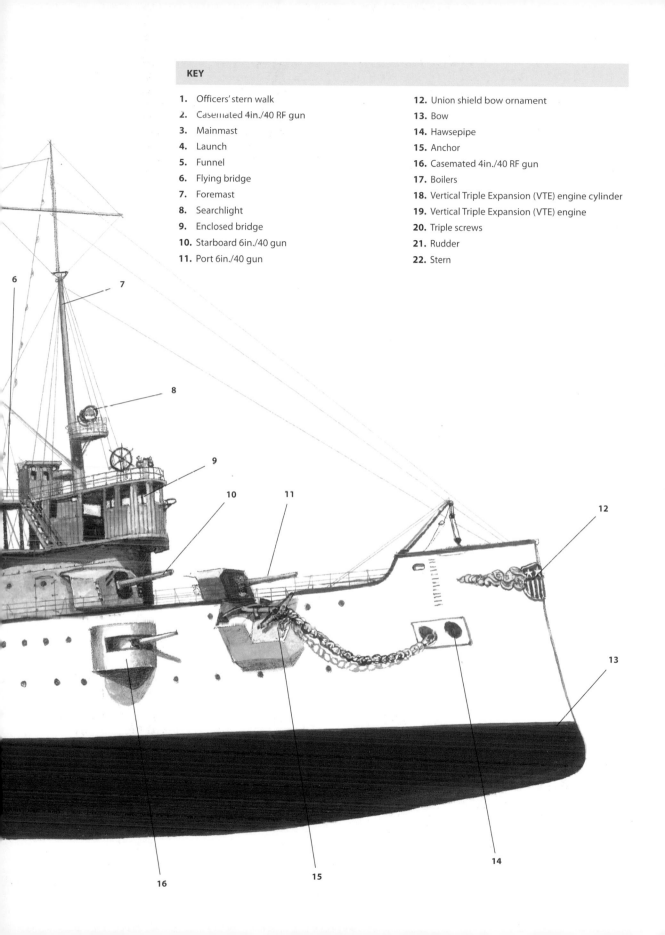

KEY

1. Officers' stern walk
2. Casemated 4in./40 RF gun
3. Mainmast
4. Launch
5. Funnel
6. Flying bridge
7. Foremast
8. Searchlight
9. Enclosed bridge
10. Starboard 6in./40 gun
11. Port 6in./40 gun
12. Union shield bow ornament
13. Bow
14. Hawsepipe
15. Anchor
16. Casemated 4in./40 RF gun
17. Boilers
18. Vertical Triple Expansion (VTE) engine cylinder
19. Vertical Triple Expansion (VTE) engine
20. Triple screws
21. Rudder
22. Stern

Columbia-class cruiser *Minneapolis* running builder's trials for Philadelphia's Cramp yards, 1894. *Minneapolis'* dual broad funnels distinguish the cruiser from *Columbia*. (NHHC NH 46173)

powerful its armored fleet, or aggressive in its foreign policy."

However, once in service the Columbias proved shockingly heavy coal consumers. In 1901 the USN rated *Minneapolis* with a mere 6,300nm range at 10kts, a sobering one-fourth of the class's designed endurance. Additionally, the Columbias' specialized commerce raiding design was now well out of step with emerging USN doctrine. Consequently, *Columbia* and *Minneapolis* would both be put in ordinary in mid-1897, after just a few years of service.

However, the 1898 war with Spain caused both cruisers to be recommissioned. Although they were put to useful service in the Atlantic, they saw little combat. Upon the brief war's conclusion, *Columbia* and *Minneapolis* would be put back into reserve in early 1899, before being recommissioned as training ships in 1902. By 1907 the Columbias were thoroughly obsolete. The largest new transatlantic liners, such as Cunard's *Mauretania* and *Lusitania*, and Norddeutscher Lloyd's *Kronprinzessin Cecilie*, all reliably cruised at 24kts, outrunning the Columbias. Consequently, *Columbia* was put back into reserve between May 1907 to June 1915, while *Minneapolis* was laid up between November 1906 and July 1917. During this period both cruisers had their torpedo tubes removed, while their stern-mounted 8in. gun was replaced by a third 6in. RF gun. During World War I they mounted three 6in. guns and four 4in. guns. *Columbia* was renamed *Old Columbia* on November 17, 1921, in order to transfer the name to the recently acquired troop transport AG-9.

Columbia-class specifications (1894)	
Length	412ft
Beam	58ft, 2in.
Draft:	22ft, 7in.
Displacement	7,375 tons
Steam propulsion	triple-screw, vertical triple expansion (VTE)
	Columbia: four stacks
	Minneapolis: two stacks
Speed	22.8kts at 18,509ihp (*Columbia*)
Range	25,520nm at 10kts (design)
	6,300nm at 10kts (Minneapolis 1901)
Coal capacity	2,135 tons (design)
	1,576 tons (*Columbia* 1891)
Auxiliary sail rig	two-masted schooner
Armament	one 8in./40 BL rifle
	two 6in./40 RF guns
	eight 4in./40 RF guns
	12 6-pdr, four 1-pdr
	four .45-70 Gatling guns
	four above-surface 14in. torpedo tubes (*Columbia*)
	four above-surface 18in. torpedo tubes (*Minneapolis*)
Protection	slopes: 4in.
	flats: 2.5in.
Complement	30 officers, 429 enlisted

Columbia-class construction						
Ship	**Built at**	**Yard**	**Laid down**	**Launched**	**Commissioned**	**Fate**
Columbia (C-12)	Philadelphia, PA	William Cramp & Sons	Dec/30/1890	Jul/26/1892	Apr/23/1894	Sold Jan/26/1922
Minneapolis (C-13)	Philadelphia, PA	William Cramp & Sons	Dec/16/1891	Aug/12/1893	Dec/13/1894	Sold Aug/05/1921

OPERATIONAL HISTORY

The Squadron of Evolution

Early in 1889 the three ABC cruisers were ready to deploy. During this era, the USN's major afloat stations consisted of the North Atlantic, South Atlantic, Pacific, and Asiatic Squadrons. These were spread throughout the world, with the North Atlantic and Pacific Squadrons deploying from the US East and West Coasts respectively, and the South Atlantic and Asiatic Squadrons rotating between non-permanent and non-sovereign ports overseas.

However, the new ABCD ships would be concentrated together into a new single squadron under Commodore John G. Walker. This was the Squadron of Evolution, also known as the White Squadron for its white-painted ships. Walker immediately began training in skillful, fast-moving signals so that his ships could be maneuvered together in real-time. Walker also expected to develop USN night signaling from a mere experiment into something reliable.

The Squadron's flagship was its largest and most capable ship, *Chicago*. The three cruisers were shortly joined by the gunboat USS *Yorktown*. Together, the four steel warships sortied from New York on November 18, 1889. The Squadron's departure was attended by Secretary of the Navy Benjamin Tracy and Admiral of the Navy David Porter. The USN was becoming increasingly enlightened as to the importance of public opinion. The Squadron's immediate first destination was Boston, where 20,000 members of the public toured *Chicago*'s decks.

The Squadron then departed Boston under sail for Lisbon, Portugal. Although *Yorktown* fell a few days behind in heavy weather, the two-week voyage was a success. The reunited Squadron then sortied from Lisbon on December 31 for several weeks of Walker's first attempt at "exercis[ing] ... in squadron tactics under steam."

The Squadron then called at Gibraltar and Cartagena, Spain in mid-January, 1890. Spanish officers touring the American ships voiced "their favorable opinions regarding the handsome construction, clean state, and the latest sea and war improvements and perfect order of the four ships." Walker's Squadron then visited Menorca's Port Mahon, followed by Toulon and Villefranche in France, and then reached Spezia, Italy on March 3. By now, two months of tactical training had inspired much improvement in the Squadron as a whole, Walker reporting: "[the] ships were much better handled, and the maneuvers were more satisfactory than ever before, showing that experience only is required to make the exercises all that is wished."

A rare view of the Squadron of Evolution under sail, likely during its initial transatlantic voyage in 1889. The photograph is from *Chicago* with *Boston*, *Atlanta*, and finally *Yorktown* in view from front to back. (NHHC NH 84527)

USS *Boston* in drydock at the New York Naval Yard, 1888. The lack of white paint shows *Boston* before the Squadron of Evolution. (NHHC NH 56526)

USS *Boston* steaming off San Francisco after being transferred to the Pacific in 1892. *Boston* would shortly be transferred to the Asiatic station where the cruiser would participate in the May 1, 1898 Battle of Manila Bay. (NHHC NH 73387)

The Squadron of Evolution then called at Corfu, Greece. Unlike the USN's usual port calls, Walker's visit to Corfu was made not for exchanging diplomatic pleasantries, but specifically in search of better weather to further train his squadron. Walker even refused the American consul's pleas to visit Athens, as its Piraeus harbor did not provide training facilities as advantageous as Corfu.

After departing Corfu, *Atlanta* and *Boston* briefly detached to Messina, Italy for drydock maintenance. *Chicago* and *Yorktown* arrived in Malta on April 17, 1890 and were joined days later by *Atlanta* and *Boston*. Although the Squadron had only been victualled through June, and over 100 sailors' enlistments were due to expire, Walker received an unexpected April 28 telegram from the US government requesting he keep the Squadron in the Mediterranean indefinitely. Several days' later the Squadron reached Algiers where a second telegram ordered him to head for Brazil, but without explanation. An increasingly irritated Walker duly stopped first at Gibraltar to pick up more supplies before briefly stopping by Tangiers, Madeira, Porto Grande, St Vincent, and Cape Verde, issuing frustrated telegrams to the Navy Department along the way. Finally, in early June, Walker dispatched *Yorktown* to New York before heading for Brazil with *Chicago*, *Atlanta*, and *Boston*.

In fact, Brazil had just overthrown Emperor Dom Pedro II's 58-year-old government, and Walker's Squadron of Evolution was intended to keep an eye on the developing political situation. However, the new Brazilian government went to great lengths to greet the arriving Squadron with enthusiasm, and by July 1890, Walker's Squadron of Evolution had returned to New York.

In a diplomatic maneuver, the Squadron was dispatched on a brief mission to Haiti in April 1891, then returned to the United States where it toured East Coast ports. By August 1891, the Squadron had grown to temporarily include cruiser *Newark* and gunboats *Bennington* and *Concord*. However, *Boston* and *Yorktown* were detached to the Pacific station in October. Walker's Squadron, now down to *Chicago*, *Atlanta*, and *Bennington*, deployed to Montevideo in January 1892. The dwindling Squadron returned to the US East Coast in May, engaged in summer exercises, and on September 9, 1892 was absorbed into the North Atlantic Squadron.

The Spanish–American War, 1898

The Spanish–American War of 1898 has considerably longer and more complicated origins than space and scope allow here. Suffice to say, the mysterious February 15, 1898 explosion of the US battleship *Maine*, anchored in Havana, simply brought Spanish–American tensions to a head, rather than inaugurating them. The *Maine* disaster made an already inevitable conflict an easy formality, and in late April 1898, Spain and the United States exchanged mutual declarations of war. Every cruiser covered in this book participated in the Spanish–American War apart from *Atlanta* and *Chicago*, which were both out of service in long overhauls.

Battle of Manila Bay, May 1, 1898

Unlike the Spaniards, the USN and its fleet were ready to fight. In October 1897, Under Secretary of the Navy Theodore Roosevelt had appointed the popular and aggressive Commodore George Dewey to command the China-based US Asiatic Squadron. Expecting war, on February 25, 1898 Roosevelt ordered the Asiatic Squadron to Hong Kong and to stay ready for offensive action against the Spanish-occupied Philippines. The inbound *Baltimore* had been scheduled to replace flagship *Olympia*, which was to return to the United States, but with war looming Roosevelt ordered *Olympia* to remain. *Baltimore* arrived in Hong Kong on April 21. Dewey's squadron now consisted of cruisers *Olympia*, *Boston*, *Baltimore*, and *Raleigh*, gunboats *Concord* and *Petrel*, armed revenue cutter *Hugh McCulloch*, and supply ships *Nanshan* and *Zafiro*. On April 23, British authorities declared their neutrality and ordered Dewey to leave Hong Kong, in accordance with international law. The Asiatic Squadron, "America's bold but lonely fleet," promptly sortied for the Philippines. Speed was limited to 8kts to save coal. Although Dewey was confident, he understood he was heading into battle 5,000nm from Honolulu, the nearest friendly port. Accompanying Dewey aboard the flagship was Captain Charles V. Gridley, *Olympia*'s deathly ill but much-loved skipper.

Awaiting Dewey in the Philippines was Contraalmirante Patricio Montojo y Pasarón. Montojo's Spanish squadron comprised his flagship, unprotected cruiser *Reina Cristina*, as well as unprotected cruisers *Castilla*, *Don Juan de Austria*, *Don Antonio de Ulloa*, *Isla de Luzon*, and *Isla de Cuba*, and gunboat *Marques del Duero*. Not only did Dewey far exceed Montojo in firepower, but the Spanish ships were also badly maintained, their crews poorly trained, and Spanish morale was low. However, Manila Bay was ringed with coastal artillery, and defended by naval mines.

Even so, Montojo knew he was horribly outmatched. He positioned his ships close to land, where his men could swim ashore, but out of supporting range of his coastal guns, which were mounted near populated areas. It appears Montojo's tactics were to minimize fatalities aboard both his ships and in the neighboring city of Manila, rather than truly attempting to repulse the attacking US squadron.

From van to rear, Dewey's column comprised *Olympia*, *Baltimore*, *Raleigh*, *Petrel*, *Concord*, *Boston*, *Hugh McCulloch*, *Nanshan*, and *Zafiro*. *Olympia* led the way, Dewey explaining: "If there are any mines in our path, the flagship will clear them away for you." *Olympia* penetrated the Boca Grande channel on April 30 at 2300hrs. At 0015hrs, May 1, El Fraile island's six rapid-firing guns opened up on the Americans, but they were silenced by American return fire.

Olympia delivers a salute at Hong Kong. *Olympia* spent the most famous part of its naval career as flagship of the Asiatic station, which had no single home port. (NHHC NH 84574)

USS *BOSTON* AT THE BATTLE OF MANILA BAY, MAY 1, 1898

On April 30, 1898, Asiatic Squadron commander Commodore George Dewey sent *Boston* and *Concord* ahead of the rest of the Asiatic Squadron to reconnoiter Luzon's deep-water Subic Bay. No Spanish warships were present, meaning they were almost certainly lying at the much larger and shallower Manila Bay, still 70nm away. Late in the day the rest of Dewey's squadron caught up with *Boston* and *Concord* at Subic Bay. Dewey's recombined squadron assembled in column and resumed the voyage south in the darkening night. After closing to within 30nm of Manila Bay, Dewey ordered all ships to general quarters. Hereafter, each ship was lit only by a single stern lantern to guide the next ship astern. Unfortunately, revenue cutter *Hugh McCulloch* was using "a Japanese brand of coal" and the "smokestack appeared like a bonfire at election time."

At 0200hrs, May 1, *Boston*'s Captain Frank Wildes ordered his gunners to catch a few hours of sleep, as action was imminent. From here on, Dewey's squadron crept southwards at just 4kts so that the Americans would penetrate Manila Bay just as dawn was breaking. Three Spanish coastal batteries in Manila uselessly opened fire at the Americans from a range of over five miles. Only *Boston* and *Concord* returned fire, each just twice at the Luneta battery, the only battery positioned where US shells could fall long without damaging the city.

A week earlier, as Dewey's Asiatic Squadron had departed Hong Kong, the captain of the Royal Navy's HMS *Immortalité* had called out to *Boston*'s skipper, "You will surely win. I have seen too much of your target practice to doubt it." Now, with the battle developing, Dewey ordered *Boston* to focus on *Reina Cristina* and *Castilla*. A *Boston* gunner recalled, "We went as close to them as we might with any degree of prudence, steaming in an ellipse and firing the port battery. Then we ported our helm and gave them the starboard guns." However, Spanish fire struck *Boston* several times. According to *Boston* eyewitnesses, Captain Wildes:

"was on the bridge, with sun helmet, palm-leaf fan, and cigar, when the shot hit the foremast three feet over his head, passed from starboard to port, cutting a shroud in the fore-rigging, and burst ten feet from the side, the recoil sending the base-plug back on deck. The captain watched the shell's progress intently, and then resumed his smoking. Of all the officers on the bridge he was the only one who did not try to dodge the missile. He simply said, "We were lucky, gentlemen!" This shell went through the foremast, making a clean hole, and a piece of the mast fell on a man's foot, but so gently as not to injure him."

The Chinese servants aboard *Boston* were pressed into service to pass ammunition, as an eyewitness reported: "The Chinese showed as much nerve as the Americans. Their faces were as impassive as when they were serving dinner in Hong Kong ... when some man would sing out from the ports that we had struck a Spanish ship they were as happy as we."

Boston had "buttoned up" for battle, closing all hatches and watertight doors; even the valves controlling artificial ventilation had been closed. Because of the fire danger, no drafts could be allowed, causing the air to become stale. The humid, tropical sunshine was hot enough above decks, but the heat of the boilers and engines, in unventilated compartments, meant it was far more stifling inside. During the battle, *Boston* recorded a below decks temperature of 116 degrees F.

Within a few hours the Americans had secured victory. *Boston* had been hit four times by Spanish shells, and a fire briefly started on board. *Boston*'s boats had been wrecked during the battle by the shock of its own battery. A single combat injury was reported aboard *Boston*; a mast splinter from the shell that just missed Captain Wildes had punctured the cheek of a quartermaster on the bridge.

Five years earlier, *Boston* had been instrumental in the eventual annexation of Hawai'i to the United States. When Hawai'i's local white plantation elite overthrew the ruling Hawai'ian dynasty, its new self-styled Provisional Government expected immediate annexation by the United States and requested an American landing party be put ashore. The main American diplomat in Hawai'i, John L. Stevens, directed *Boston* to land an armed party to protect supposedly threatened American civilians. *Boston* landed a total of 162 marines and naval infantry the afternoon of January 16, 1893, helping secure the American-friendly Provisional Government. However, in March 1893, before Hawai'i could be formally annexed, Democrat Grover Cleveland assumed the US Presidency. Cleveland was an anti-imperialist who condemned the overthrow of the royal Hawai'ian government and refused to annex the archipelago during his term in office. The new island government conducted its affairs as the independent Republic of Hawai'i until a friendlier Republican administration annexed Hawai'i in 1898.

In 1918 *Boston* was ultimately converted to a receiving ship at Yerba Buena Island in San Francisco Bay, serving in that capacity as the renamed *Despatch* until 1940. The cruiser then served as a radio school between 1940 and 1945 before being scuttled off San Francisco in 1946.

Olympia's 36-star US naval ensign as flown from the flagship during the May 1, 1898 Battle of Manila Bay. The reverse of the hoist is stamped "U.S.S. OLYMPIA MANILA BAY MAY 1 1898." (NHHC 1963-318-A)

Commodore Dewey's position immortalized on the flying bridge above Olympia's armored conning tower, August 2022. There was no designed armored command post for admirals aboard US protected cruisers, an arrangement one suspects glory-seeking admirals preferred. (Author)

By 0515hrs, May 1, Dewey's squadron was in sight in the early daylight off Manila. Montojo's Spanish squadron was likewise visible huddling motionless off Manila Bay's southern shoreline. Dewey, standing in the open directly above Olympia's conning tower, signaled, "Prepare for general action." Spanish ships and coastal batteries opened fire. However, no shells connected as the Americans were still well out of range. At 0541hrs, after closing within 5,500yds of Montojo's squadron, Dewey announced through a voicepipe to Olympia's captain, one deck beneath him in Olympia's conning tower: "You may fire when ready, Gridley."

The Americans, passing from east to west, opened fire from their port guns while cruising at 6–8kts. After two miles, Dewey reversed course and exercised his starboard batteries against the Spaniards, closing to 2,000–3,000yds. Although not obvious to the Americans, they were scoring heavy damage on the Spanish ships. Olympia sank a small Spanish boat and drove another aground, mistakenly believing these were torpedo boats making attacks.

During Dewey's fifth firing pass, Captain Gridley seemed to report that Olympia had only 15 5in. rounds left per gun. At 1935hrs Dewey led the US squadron out of range to confer with his ship captains, ordering his crews to have breakfast. It was then that Dewey discovered that the original message had been in error. Rather than there only being 15 rounds remaining per gun, only 15 rounds had been fired per gun.

But the Spanish were already defeated. Montojo's flagship Reina Cristina was so badly hammered that Montojo gave the order for scuttling. Don Antonio de Ulloa had sunk, Castilla was ablaze and abandoned, and Isla de Luzon and Marques del Duero had suffered damage. Montojo ordered all ships capable of doing so back into Bacoor Bay, and then to scuttle themselves and surrender once they were no longer capable of fighting.

At 1156hrs the Americans renewed their attack, with Olympia's place in the vanguard taken by Baltimore. Now well ahead of the rest, Baltimore furiously engaged the Canacao Battery and Fort Sangley, silencing them after ten minutes.

Montojo and the Spanish fort at Cavite shortly surrendered. They had suffered 381 killed during the battle. American fire had been highly destructive, despite a hit rate of 1–2 percent, typical for the era. In contrast, Dewey reported nine wounded and no fatalities, although the chief engineer of Hugh McColloch had died of a heart attack moments before the battle. The US squadron anchored just offshore, despite many intact Spanish shore batteries. That evening an uneasy truce reigned, with Olympia's band serenading Manilans with music, including numerous Spanish pieces. In the background, burning Spanish ships continued to occasionally cook off their magazines. As one account observes, "It was a strange end to a strange day."

Guam, Hawai'i, and Manila

On June 20, 1898, *Charleston* sailed into Guam's Agana harbor. *Charleston* fired several 3lb shells at the dilapidated Spanish fort supposedly defending Guam, kicking off a two-day comedy of errors that resulted in no casualties on either side and the Guam garrison's surrender to the Americans the following morning. As it turned out, Guam was practically defenseless and its men had been unaware Spain and the United States were even at war.

Meanwhile, *Philadelphia* had been dispatched from San Francisco to formalize the annexation of Hawai'i. This was accomplished on August 12. By then *Charleston* had long departed Guam. The cruiser had arrived at Manila Bay on June 30, where she reinforced Dewey's Asiatic Squadron blockade. Together, Dewey's original Manila Bay force, plus *Charleston*, engaged in the final August 13 bombardment of Manila. This operation was actually a secret political sham with the Spanish that shortly went awry. Nevertheless, Manila promptly surrendered to the Americans, as had been secretly agreed beforehand.

Cruiser *Charleston* at Hong Kong in 1898. *Charleston* is wearing wartime overall haze gray, meaning this photograph was likely taken almost immediately after the end of the Spanish–American War. *Charleston* foundered off Luzon the following year. (NHHC NH 61939)

Actions in the Atlantic and Caribbean

No US protected cruisers were present at Santiago, Cuba on July 3, 1898, meaning the decisive naval battle of the Atlantic and Caribbean theater was won by battleships, armored cruisers, and gunboats. Nevertheless, US protected cruisers participated in the overall Cuba and Puerto Rico blockades, as well as defensive patrols of the US East Coast.

Newark was recommissioned in May 1898 and assigned to the Cuba blockade. The cruiser shot up the wrecks of the Spanish shattered fleet after Santiago, then participated in the bombardment of Manzanillo on August 12. Throughout the Spanish–American War, *San Francisco* patrolled off Florida and Cuba.

On March 15, 1898 *Columbia* was recommissioned. The cruiser was shortly assigned to Commodore Winfield Scott Schley's Flying Squadron, but was then detached to the Northern Patrol Squadron, which patrolled the New England coast in the event Cervera's squadron appeared. Joining *Columbia* was *Minneapolis*, which scouted as far south as Venezuela searching for Cervera.

A Murat Halstead painting of cruiser USS *Columbia* on night patrol during the 1898 Spanish–American War. *Columbia* and *Minneapolis* were useful for scouting, but they were so expensive to operate that they were difficult to justify during peacetime. (Public Domain)

Columbia was then largely relegated to convoy operations, but beginning in July the cruiser assisted in the ongoing blockade and occupation of Puerto Rico. Then, on the night of August 8, 1898, *Columbia* finally saw action when the cruiser shelled advancing Spanish troops at the Fajardo lighthouse. A global cease-fire was declared on August 12, 1898, essentially ending the Spanish–American War.

Final operations 1899–1923

By 1899 the USN forces afloat consisted of the North Atlantic station, Pacific station, and Asiatic station. Many US protected cruisers engaged in the

1899–1902 Philippine–American War, the Filipino insurgency that erupted when the United States unilaterally occupied the Philippines in 1898. US protected cruisers' primary duties were to support US troops ashore with naval gunfire, as well as landing naval infantry parties when required. However, *Charleston* was wrecked beyond repair off Luzon on November 2, 1899.

In addition to the Philippine–American War, US protected cruisers functioned in countless gunboat diplomacy missions in the Caribbean, in Latin

G USS *BALTIMORE* (C-3) LAYING THE NORTH SEA MINE BARRAGE, 1918

Early in World War I, Britain's Admiralty had conceived an idea to lay a massive naval mine barrage in the North Sea to choke off German U-boat sorties. The British soon cooled on this idea, but by 1917 certain USN figures had enthusiastically adopted it. By its 1918 execution, the Americans were considerably more enthusiastic about the idea. By October 1917, American plans were to manufacture 125,000 mines, convert eight merchantmen to minelayers, and organize 24 cargo ships to transport mines to Scotland, where they would be deployed by several dedicated flotillas. The USN officials convinced the now-reluctant Admiralty to join them in a combined Anglo-American minelaying operation. Rear Admiral Lewis Clinton-Baker, who was in charge of British minelaying, called the North Sea mine barrage, "The biggest mine-planting stunt in history."

The US Navy and Royal Navy commenced laying the barrage in March 1918. Of the planned 270nm of the barrage, the USN was expected to lay 190nm, with the overall barrage 15–35nm wide. The mining force's main bases were at Inverness and Invergordon in Scotland.

Baltimore is seen laying mines during one of the 1918 North Sea expeditions. *Baltimore*'s mines were laid via a davit on the mainmast, which swung out 90 degrees and laid the mines over the side of the hull. *Baltimore* was joined in the Mining Force by *San Francisco*, which had been equipped to carry 170 mines, while *Baltimore* could carry 180. Captain Reginald Belknap commanded Mining Squadron 1, which was based in Inverness. An American mine-planting expedition would include all ten minelayers, escorted by US or British warships, and would lay a total of about 5,000 mines in four hours.

The mine barrage had not yet been completed by the November 1918 armistice. Nevertheless, the Americans had laid 56,000 mines, or 80 percent of the Anglo-American total. After the war, the North Sea barrage was officially credited with a mere four U-boats sunk – two probably sunk, and two possibly sunk. Another eight were certainly damaged, and the barrage may have sunk another five U-boats. Postwar evaluations of the barrage considered it ineffective, although it may have seriously affected German morale and intentions.

For better or worse, *Baltimore* played a central role in many historical American events. *Baltimore*'s dance with American history began many years earlier in 1890, when *Baltimore* returned the remains of *Monitor* designer John Ericsson to his native Sweden.

Baltimore was the central player in the 1891 Chilean crisis, which is also known as the *Baltimore* Affair. Since its victory in the 1879–84 War of the Pacific, Chile had increasingly emerged as a military and political rival to the United States in the Pacific coastal region of Latin America . This was further driven home by Chile's acquisition of state-of-the-art protected cruiser *Esmeralda*, which was used to intimidate outmatched US naval forces in Panama in 1885. Such incidents contributed to the US naval build-up that began in the 1880s.

Protected cruiser *Baltimore* was one of the immediate results of this build-up. In 1891, the cruiser happened to make a port call at Valparaíso, Chile. *Baltimore* was then commanded by Captain Winfield Scott Schley, who would later contribute to the controversy at the 1898 Battle of Santiago. On October 16, 1891, while a group of *Baltimore* sailors were on shore leave at Valparaíso's True Blue Saloon, a *Baltimore* seaman spat at a portrait of the Chilean national hero Arturo Prat. A riot broke out, and the Chilean mob ultimately left two US sailors dead and 17 injured. Over 30 *Baltimore* sailors were arrested by the local Chilean police. The US government demanded reparations, and after much diplomatic sparring between the two governments, Chile paid the United States $75,000 in gold to absolve itself of the matter. Regardless of the dubious behavior of the US sailors and government, Chile's concession openly reveals that the United States had surpassed the naval strength of its former rival.

Baltimore was decommissioned at Pearl Harbor in 1922 and converted into a receiving ship. Present during the December 7, 1941 Pearl Harbor attack, *Baltimore* was finally towed to sea and scuttled on September 22, 1944.

Chicago viewed at the New York Naval Yard in Brooklyn, c.1899–1900. Chicago has not received the standard white peacetime US paint and is clearly in the middle of an overhaul. (LOC LC-D4-32266)

America, and in East Asia. Just one example of this was on December 7, 1903, when the Pacific-based *Boston* arrived off Panama to help bolster Panamanian declarations of independence from Colombia. Of course, American-backed Panamanian independence came with the caveat of American rights to build and operate the planned Panama Canal.

By the early 20th century, the USN's protected cruisers were rapidly becoming obsolete. They were increasingly allocated to auxiliary roles or laid up for periods in reserve. *Philadelphia* was converted into a receiving ship at the Puget Sound Naval Yard in 1904. In January 1905 *Atlanta* was removed from front-line duty and spent the next seven years in training and barracks ship duties until being struck on April 24, 1912. The USN decommissioned *Newark* in June 1913, relinquishing the cruiser to the US Public Health Service as a quarantine hulk.

The United States then entered World War I against Germany in April 1917. This involved a massive reorganization of combat units, and the recommissioning of the most useful protected cruisers into patrol, escort, or auxiliary roles. Protected cruisers *Columbia*, *Minneapolis*, and *Olympia* were concentrated in the Atlantic for East Coast patrol duties in 1917, followed by transatlantic escort duty with the Cruiser and Transport Force in 1918. *Columbia* made five transatlantic voyages as a convoy escort in 1918, while *Minneapolis* completed four. In April 1918, *Olympia* was given a special mission as part of the Russia Intervention. After arriving in Murmansk in June, *Olympia* helped support the occupation of Archangelsk against the Bolsheviks.

Several older protected cruisers served in wartime auxiliary roles. *Chicago* was recommissioned in April 1917 and named flagship Atlantic Submarine Force. Meanwhile, *San Francisco* and *Baltimore* were assigned to the US Mine Force in 1918, as they had been converted to cruiser-minelayers in 1911 and 1915 respectively. *San Francisco* and *Baltimore* participated in the 1918 North Sea minelaying operations through to the end of the war.

Columbia was transferred to the Atlantic Fleet's Destroyer Force in 1919 and cruised off the US East Coast for the next two years. In early February 1919, *Minneapolis* arrived at San Diego as the Pacific station flagship. Joining *Minneapolis* in the Pacific was cruiser *Chicago*, which was assigned submarine tender duty at Pearl Harbor.

Minneapolis is seen in World War I-era dazzle camouflage in 1918. World War I was the last hurrah of the US protected cruisers, as they were all removed from service in the early 1920s as anything other than decommissioned auxiliaries. (NHHC NH 46198)

The last notable mission of a US protected cruiser was in late 1921, when *Olympia* transported the Americans' designated Unknown Soldier home to the United States from France. With major naval cuts looming, the USN permanently decommissioned *Minneapolis*, *Columbia*, and *San Francisco* in 1921; *Baltimore* and *Olympia* in 1922; and finally *Chicago* in 1923. The era of the US protected cruiser was over.

The preserved *Olympia*

On June 30, 1931, the USN redesignated *Olympia* as IX-40 (Miscellaneous, Unclassified No. 40). On September 11, 1957, the USN turned *Olympia* over to the Cruiser Olympia Society, a non-profit organization founded to preserve *Olympia* and operate the cruiser as a museum and memorial in Philadelphia. *Olympia* was dry docked at this time, but lack of funds meant little refurbishment could be done. However, the Society began returning *Olympia*'s appearance to the Manila Bay configuration. Full-scale steel mock-ups of *Olympia*'s long gone 8in. turrets and guns were reconstructed, as were replica masts and fighting tops. Replacement guns for *Olympia*'s removed 5in. battery were located and remounted. *Olympia* was repainted back to the Victorian-era livery of white hull, buff upper works, and black gun barrels.

In 1976 the US federal government named *Olympia* a National Historic Landmark. By 1995 the Cruiser Olympia Society had proposed merging its organization with Philadelphia's Independence Seaport Museum, which officially assumed control of *Olympia* on January 1, 1996. *Olympia*'s new operators immediately commenced a major long-term project to restore the cruiser.

Today, *Olympia* is the world's oldest surviving steel warship. Since 1977 the cruiser has been moored at Penn's Landing in Philadelphia. *Olympia*'s starboard engine room is still largely intact, and in 1987 the American Society of Mechanical Engineers designated *Olympia*'s surviving 1890s-era vertical triple expansion engine as a National Historic Engineering Landmark. As a former *Olympia* museum officer observed: "To stand in *Olympia*'s engine room is to be in the middle of the Industrial Revolution. It's this gorgeous piece of machinery."

Directly across the Delaware River from *Olympia* is the 1943 US battleship *New Jersey*, moored at Camden, in its namesake state. As independent entities, both warships are well preserved and available for the public to visit as separate museums. The author had the good fortune to tour the vessels back-to-back. Although *Olympia* is a cruiser and *New Jersey* a battleship, a comparison of the two is not as unwarranted as might first seem. Both are American, both were designed as flagships, both were state-of-the-art when completed, and both were arguably the finest of their types ever built. As it proved, nothing throws 1890s American naval design and philosophy into relief like touring an 1895 cruiser and 1943 battleship mere hours apart.

When exploring the two warships, the most immediate difference is that watertight integrity was not nearly as advanced or as revered in *Olympia*'s time as it had become by the 1940s. Although *Olympia* is one-tenth *New Jersey*'s size, *Olympia*'s sheltered gun deck feels open and airy compared to *New Jersey*, the tight (but austere) passageways of which feel claustrophobic. *Olympia* has many portholes, open casemates, and considerable amounts of wood furnishing, all of which are virtually absent aboard *New Jersey*. Many of *Olympia*'s enlisted men slept in hammocks hung nightly

The preserved cruiser *Olympia* seen at Penn's Landing in Philadelphia, August 2022. *Olympia* is the ward of the Independence Seaport Museum, the main building of which is just out of frame to the right. (Author)

from the overhead on the gun deck, where there is reasonable air and light, while *New Jersey*'s modern-style steel bunks are well below decks, with all the air coming from forced ventilation (and later air conditioning). In *Olympia*'s time the crew also messed where they bunked, whereas *New Jersey*'s men messed in dedicated cafeteria-style areas in the modern tradition. *Olympia*'s officers were also allowed limited alcohol, whereas the USN had banned alcohol entirely by 1943. Finally, *Olympia*'s admiral's stateroom is considerably larger and more luxurious than its *New Jersey* counterpart. Although this derives partly from Victorian sensibilities, a major factor is that 1890s admirals (particularly on the Asiatic station) were expected to be as much diplomats as they were squadron commanders.

ABOVE LEFT
Olympia's armored conning tower, foremast, and fighting top viewed from the starboard weather deck, August 2022. *Olympia*'s mast and fighting top have been reconstructed from the original. (Author)

ABOVE RIGHT
A view of *Olympia* from the bow, displaying the conning tower, bridge, and reconstructed forward 8in. gun turret, August 2022. *Olympia* is currently moored alongside the World War II-era submarine *Becuna* at Penn's Landing, Philadelphia. (Author)

However, upon diving below decks, *Olympia* turns out to be a much more cramped and visibly dangerous place to work than *New Jersey*. Compared to the battleship, *Olympia*'s overheads are low and often cluttered, as the placement of equipment and machinery was not designed for 20th-century ideas of crew safety and ergonomics. This is borne out by the surprisingly high number of shipboard casualties *Olympia* suffered during normal peacetime operations.

Certain technologies evolved little between 1895 and 1943. The warships' respective armored conning towers are immediately recognizable to each other. In battle, both *Olympia* and *New Jersey* were conned through narrow eye slits cut through the conning tower's thick cylindrical armored shell. *Olympia*'s conning tower is just large enough for the captain and the helm, whereas *New Jersey*'s conning tower is larger, equipped with additional instrumentation, and just large enough for multiple personnel. However, although *New Jersey*'s armor is four times thicker, the battleship's 1943-era Krupp armor was not, inch-for-inch, significantly more efficient than the 1890s Harvey armor of *Olympia*.

CONCLUSION

US protected cruisers were the embryo of the modern, steel-constructed US Navy that exists today. The May 1, 1898 Battle of Manila Bay instantly ushered in the era of US globalism. More specifically, by putting the United States in the Philippines, it set in motion a 43-year chain of events that would directly lead to the United States' entry into World War II. Manila Bay is therefore one of the most decisive battles in history, and it was won essentially by US protected cruisers.

Perhaps most importantly, the earliest US protected cruisers inaugurated a new technological era in the United States. They were the catalyst for the beginning of a peacetime military–industrial complex. Before *Atlanta*, *Boston*, and *Chicago*, the US economy, however strong in raw terms, was often plagued by industries that were comparatively primitive compared with their most advanced counterparts in Europe. Such inferiorities led to notions of American provincialism and backwardness, both in the United States and in Europe. But after the American revolution in high-grade steel production, American society would increasingly expect all of its industries to be the best in the world.

SELECT BIBLIOGRAPHY

The Story of Our Wonderful Victories, Told by Dewey, Schley, Wheeler, and Other Heroes, (1899), Nabu Press (2012)

Alden, Commander John. T., *The American Steel Navy*, Naval Institute Press, (2008)

Bennett, Passed Assistant Engineer Frank M., *The Steam Navy of the United States: A History of the Growth of the Steam Vessel of War in the U.S. Navy, and of the Naval Engineer Corps,* (1896), Nabu Press (2012)

Burr, Lawrence, *US Cruisers 1883–1904: The Birth of the Steel Navy*, Osprey Publishing, (2008)

Chesneau, Roger, and Kolesnik, Eugene M. (eds), *Conway's All the World's Fighting Ships 1860–1905*, Mayflower Books, (1979)

Cooling, Benjamin Franklin, *Benjamin Franklin Tracy: Father of the Modern American Fighting Navy*, Archon Books, (1973)

Cooling, Benjamin Franklin, *Gray Steel and Blue Water Navy: The Formative Years of America's Military–Industrial Complex 1881–1917*, Archon Books, (1979)

Cooling, Benjamin Franklin, *USS Olympia: Herald of Empire*, Naval Institute Press, (2000)

DeOrsay, Paul B., *Project Update: Cruiser Olympia*, Independence Seaport Museum. Philadelphia, Pennsylvania, (1997)

Evans, Joel C., "The Battle of Manila Bay – The Destruction of the Spanish Fleet as Told by Eye-Witnesses, Part IV, Narrative of the Gunner of the BOSTON," *The Century Vol. 56, No. 4,* The Century Company, New York, (1898)

Friedman, Norman, *U.S. Cruisers: An Illustrated Design History*, Naval Institute Press, (1984)

Gardiner, Robert and Lambert, Andrew (eds), *Steam, Steel, and Shellfire: The Steam Warship 1815–1905*, Chartwell Books Inc, (2001)

Jaffe, Alan, "Will new ways to experience Olympia keep the cruiser afloat?" WHYY.org, (2016)

Leeke, Jim, *Manila and Santiago: The New Steel Navy in the Spanish–American War*, Naval Institute Press, (2009)

McBride, William M., *Technological Change and the United States Navy 1865–1945*, The Johns Hopkins University Press, (2000)

Misa, Thomas J., *A Nation of Steel: The Making of Modern America 1865–1925*, The Johns Hopkins University Press, (1995)

Preston, Antony, *Cruisers*, Bison Books Ltd, (1982)

Rentfrow, James C., *Home Squadron: The U.S. Navy on the North Atlantic Station*, Naval Institute Press, (2014)

Schulman, Mark Russell *Navalism and the Emergence of American Sea Power: 1882–1893*, Naval Institute Press, (1995)

US Department of the Navy, *Annual Reports of the US Navy*

www.spanamwar.com

http://www.navsource.org

http://www.history.navy.mil/

USS *Boston*'s crew mans the yards during the Centennial Naval Parade, April 29, 1889. *Boston* flies the four-star flag of Admiral David Dixon Porter. Porter is remembered as being an archconservative, but the reality of his tenure immediately before the Steel Navy is more nuanced. (NHHC NH 416)

INDEX

Note: All ships are cruisers unless otherwise stated.
Page locators in bold refer to plate captions,
pictures and illustrations.